PARIS ME
HANDBOO

BRIAN HARDY

Capital Transport

First published 1988

ISBN 185414 104 X

Published by Capital Transport Publishing
38 Long Elmes, Harrow Weald, Middlesex

Printed by the KPC Group, Ashford, Kent

© Capital Transport Publishing and Brian Hardy 1988

Front cover **A train of MP73 stock emerges from the tunnel near Place d'Italie on line 6, which is one of four Métro lines equipped for 'pneu' operation.** *Brian Hardy*

Back cover upper **Trains of MF67 stock on line 12 at the northern terminus of Porte de la Chapelle, both in the new blue and white livery. This station still retains much of its Nord-Sud character, even though that company ceased to exist in 1930.** *Brian Hardy*

Back cover lower **A view of a small part of the engineers' train depot at Villette showing double-ended works motor cars (Tracteurs) converted from Sprague stock. In the background can be seen a personnel carrier – a Sprague second class trailer – still in original livery.** *Brian Hardy*

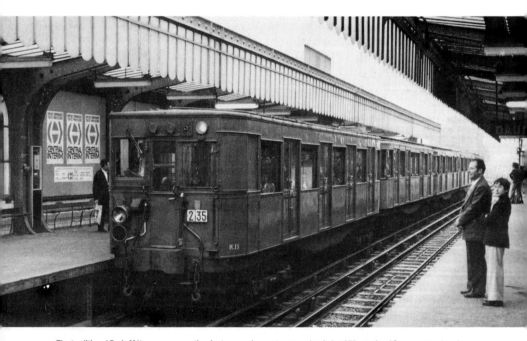

The traditional Paris Métro, as many enthusiasts may choose to remember it. In 1975, a train of Sprague stock arrives at Jaurès on line 2, heading for Nation. It is of interest to note that the train 'set' number of '235' indicates line 2, train 35, a similar formula being employed on other lines. The leading motor car of the train, M19, has origins dating back to 1900, being rebuilt in 1905, 1910, 1929 and to its final form in 1936, with four pairs of equally-spaced doors per side.

R.J. Greenaway

CONTENTS

A train of MF77 stock approaches Creteil-l'Echat on line 8, heading for the southern terminus of Creteil-Préfecture. The train on the left is one of several that can be seen stabled in off-peak periods. This additional track was originally intended to be a third, through line, to enable semi-fast services to be operated. To date, this plan has not been pursued.
Brian Hardy

AUTHOR'S NOTE

In 1970, the book 'On Rails Under Paris', written by B.J. Prigmore, was published by the then Light Railway Transport League, followed in 1974 by an updated edition. Both of these works became out of date fairly quickly, due to the rapidity with which updating, modernisation and expansion of the Paris Métro was progressing. It was the original intention to further update 'On Rails Under Paris' in the early-1980s, but publishing difficulties subsequently caused this plan to be shelved. In 1984, the writer of the original books, B.J. Prigmore – well known in electric railway organisations for his expert technical knowledge – regrettably died, and thus plans for republishing this book continued to lie dormant.

In recent months, the opportunity has arisen to once again consider publishing a book, in English, on the Paris Métro, this being the finished product. To provide a readable and informative account on such a vast subject in the 104 pages available has been a formidable task – what to include and how much and, of course, what to leave out. There is no doubt, though, that in any railway enthusiasts' movement, the main interest will be in rolling stock. However, it is right that other topics should be included and I hope this publication will appeal not only to those interested in rolling stock, but also to those with other interests in the Paris Métro. It has not been possible to include details of the RER, a system which could fill a book in its own right.

Bearing in mind that there have been extensive changes to the Paris Métro since the original two editions were published, it was thought that this book should be completely re-written and given a new title. Notwithstanding this, the author wishes to place on record his appreciation to the late B.J. Prigmore for generating a great interest in the subject, and to the LRTA, the LRTL's successor.

As always, a work of this kind is never the result of one person's efforts, and the author would like to express his sincere thanks to the following for their help, assistance and guidance with this publication: B. Patton (especially with the first two chapters) and C.S. Best (both of whom have done a magnificent job in translating various documents from French into English), W.R. Clarke (Operations Director, London Underground Limited), B.H. Steinkamp (who has willingly shared his intimate and detailed knowledge of the Paris Métro of more than 30 years), Pascal Lesure, R.J. Greenaway, D.S. Berman, D.F. Croome, J.F. Wright and J.F. Thomason. Finally, a special note of thanks is expressed to the RATP (Paris Transport Authority), especially Messieurs Guigonnet, Guibereau, Millot, Portier, Garandel, Teilhout and Billaudel, all of whom patiently assisted me with my researches and answered what must have seemed like numerous and never-ending questions, and to the Public Relations Department of the RATP for allowing me to publish this work. If, unintentionally, I have failed to acknowledge anyone else, I apologise.

The information in this book is correct to 1 June 1988, but where statistical information is quoted, this is correct, as far as is possible, to the end of 1987. Observations and suggestions for any future edition would be welcomed by the Author, via the Publisher.

This book is dedicated to the late B.J. Prigmore, and to friend and colleague Fred Ivey, both of whom nurtured my interest in the Paris Métro, far beyond the extent of what my family and I had originally envisaged!

BRIAN HARDY,

Eastcote, Middlesex.
June 1988.

CHAPTER 1
PARIS AND ITS MÉTRO – THE ORIGINS

The municipal area of the city of Paris is still defined by the line of what was, until about 1920, a ring of fortifications pierced by numerous gates. The area immediately beyond the city formed until recently the Département of the Seine but this has now been sub-divided into the Départements of Seine-Saint-Denis, Hauts-de-Seine and Val-de-Marne. The area of Greater Paris nowadays spreads even beyond this and overall planning is the responsibility of the planning commission for the Île-de-France Region.

The existence of the city walls had a psychological as well as a physical effect on the growth of the city and even as late as the 1890s, Paris had still not experienced the suburban sprawl which had already become a feature of London. The central area had, however, been greatly rebuilt and improved during the Second Empire (1852-1870), largely through the efforts of Baron Haussmann, the Préfect of the Seine. Among the improvements completed by him was the building of a central produce market, Les Halles, and the first suggestion for an urban railway was made in 1845 by one de Kérizouet, who proposed a line, to be worked by cable, to link Les Halles with the Gare du Nord and the Gare de Lyon. A similar proposal in 1856 envisaged an underground railway and was taken sufficiently seriously for the basement of Les Halles to be arranged to allow for its passage. Unfortunately, by the time a railway actually reached this spot (in the shape of the RER), Les Halles themselves had gone. In 1872 the Département of the Seine actually drew up a plan for an underground, but there were no takers for the concession. During the next decade there were various plans for elevated lines but the establishment of a network of tramways lessened the need for any more elaborate solution, at least for a time. Meanwhile, the Law of 11 June 1880 allowed local communities to build railways to serve their own areas (chemins de fer d'intérêt local) and this meant that responsibility for any purely urban railway was transferred from the Département to the City Council. The latter then produced a plan for a railway built to main line standards, but the Government pointed out that such a system would be of more than local importance and refused to grant it to the City. This was the start of a conflict which was to rumble on and off for the next thirteen years and which made most Parisians sceptical that any line would ever be built. In the course of this debate, numerous plans were drawn up, those by the Government and the main line railways envisaging something along the lines of the present RER, with the idea of extending the main lines into the centre of the city and thus linking the suburbs to the centre. Gustave Eiffel (of 'Tower' fame) and his company got in on the act and produced two plans, one of which did not please the Council and one which pleased neither side. The municipal authorities, on the other hand, wanted a system that would serve purely urban traffic flows, and to make sure that the main line companies were kept out they proposed to build to a restricted loading gauge. The municipal plans tended to centre around what ultimately became lines 2, 3 and 6 of the Métro, while they also actively supported a plan put forward by Jean-Baptiste Berlier for a tube line from Porte de Vincennes to Porte Dauphine via the route of the present line 1 for much of the way. This would have been worked by electric traction and its sharp curves and steep gradients made it the true precursor of the Métro, though it seems to have been seen more as a tramway than a railway. When Berlier was unable to raise the capital for his line, it was added to the municipal plans. The City's attitude was aptly summed up by one official who said that he wanted a Métro which belonged to the same family «qu'il puisse tutoyer».

The arguments might have gone on indefinitely had not the approach of yet another Paris exhibition, planned for 1900, concentrated the official mind wonderfully. In 1896 the municipality adopted a plan for a metre-gauge underground railway system, initially to consist of six lines, using carriages which would be only 1.9m wide. The City would build the tunnels and the platforms of the stations, but operation would be entrusted to a company which would also be responsible for laying the track, providing access to the stations and buying the rolling stock. When the concession was advertised, six tenders were received and it was finally awarded to the Compagnie Générale de Traction, which was headed by a Belgian financier, the Baron Empain. Its engineers insisted that both the loading and track gauges be widened and to this the City reluctantly agreed. When the proposal went before the central government, the track gauge was further widened to standard (1.435m) at the request of the Minister of Defence, and the width of the carriages was also increased to 2.40m. The municipality again had to give way, though it was able to comfort itself with noting that this loading gauge would still be too narrow to allow the passage of main line trains. With these amendments agreed, the plan was authorised by the Law of 30 March 1898. The CGT then went on to form a limited company, the Compagnie du Chemin de Fer Métropolitain de Paris, normally (and henceforth) referred to as the CMP. This company had a capital of 25 million Francs. The City meanwhile had also raised a loan and, by an inspired stroke, entrusted the building of the system to an Engineer of the Public Works Board for Roads and Bridges, Fulgence Bienvenüe. He had graduated as a Civil Engineer from the Polytechnique in 1870 and had since then acquired much experience of railway building in difficult terrain as well as laying out some of the tramways in Paris. In 1896 he had just finished work on some aqueducts and had then become involved with the preliminary plans for the Métro. Thanks to his energy and drive, and to the opening up of entire streets at a time, the building of the Métro went ahead with amazing speed, particularly remarkable when compared with the prolonged debates about its planning. Work on line 1 began in November 1898 and it was opened for traffic without ceremony at 13.00 on 19 July 1900. At first there were only ten three-car trains in service and by the time this was increased two months later, a proper system of signalling was in operation. It soon became evident that the Métro was going to be far more successful than anyone had dared to hope, since the number of passengers carried rose from 1.8 million in August to almost 4 million in December. Thus encouraged, the City pressed ahead with the building of new lines to such effect that the original network was completed more than a year ahead of schedule in January 1910, only to be inundated immediately by severe flooding which affected most lines from January to April 1910.

Long before this date, however, plans for more extensions had already been made. Bienvenüe was consistently aware of the need to plan the system as a whole – in his words «Le Métro ne se refait pas» – ('the Métro wouldn't happen again') – and it was therefore important that the planning should be governed by long- as well as short-term considerations. In 1901 he submitted a plan for various extensions and for two new lines, the predecessors of lines 9 and 10. Two additional lines, mentioned as possibilities in the original agreement, were authorised in April 1902 (line 7) and April 1903 (line 8). The result of this advance planning was that some important and difficult works, such as the crossing of lines 3, 7 and 8 at Opéra (all underground) could be carried out as one combined operation, even though part of them would not be needed for some years to come.

But the progress of the CMP was not made in the security of a complete monopoly. Berlier (q.v. above) had not given up his interest in building a tube line and in 1901 he and one Janicot obtained from the City a concession for such a line from Montmartre to Montparnasse, which they immediately made over to the Société du Chemin de Fer Électrique Souterrain Nord-Sud de Paris, usually (and again, henceforth) called the Nord-Sud for short. The main difference between this and the CMP's concession was that the Nord-Sud lines were to be built at the company's own expense. It was intended that, being in tube, they would not have to follow the street pattern, but the waterlogged subsoil of Paris was a totally different proposition from the London clay, and after a few trial borings it was decided that the Nord-Sud would have to be built by conventional Parisian methods. Construction of the main line was authorised in 1905 (line A) along with an extension to Porte de Versailles and a branch (line B) from the Gare Saint-Lazare to Porte de Saint-Ouen. Further extensions and a third line from Montparnasse to Porte de Vanves (line C) were authorised between 1908 and 1912.

While in many ways the lines of the Nord-Sud resembled very closely those of the CMP, the stations were more spacious with decorations of mosaic patterns and improved lighting. But the biggest difference was in the system of current collection. To avoid the problem of voltage drop without the building of too many substations, the Nord-Sud was electrified on a three-wire 1,200V system. The leading motor coach of a train picked up current at +600V from an overhead wire via a small pantograph (which folded sideways when not in use), while the rear motor took current at –600V from a third rail. In an emergency, both could operate from either pick-up at 600V only. Line A followed a particularly tortuous course and there were many difficulties encountered in building it, especially in the hilly area around Montmartre; it abounded in sharp curves and steep gradients (which used to produce marvellous sound effects from the Nord-Sud and later the Classic stock). The first section did not open until 1910. Fares were the same as on the CMP and transfer facilities were made freely available between the two systems.

Meanwhile, the plan for Bienvenüe's additional network «réseau complémentaire» had been adopted by the City, and it was authorised in 1910. As soon as work on the original lines had finished, it began on the new ones and continued unabated until 1914, and then at a slower pace until 1916. Apart from a brief suspension of services on some lines in the autumn of 1914, the main effect of the First World War on the CMP was the development of a system of electropneumatic closing of the doors, which allowed a reduction of the crews on a five-coach train from six to four.

The immediate inter-war years brought many difficulties in the form of rising costs and demands for shorter working hours by the crews. The first strike on the Métro and the first fares increase came in 1919, despite which the CMP was in 1920 unable to pay to the City the money due under the Law of 1898. After much discussion, therefore, new agreements were drawn up between the municipality and the two companies, under which the former undertook financial responsibility for the operation of both systems (the CMP and the Nord-Sud), the companies receiving in return a fixed price of 1.7 centimes for each ticket issued. As the Département of the Seine had just bought up the various tramway companies (which included the Compagnie Générale des Omnibus), local Government was now firmly in control of the city's transport. The only trouble was that the Métro was controlled by the City, whereas the newly-created Société des Transports en Commune de la Région Parisienne was under the Département of the Seine, and it was much better placed to compete with the Métro than the individual companies had been. During the 1920s, when traffic was continually growing at a rate fast enough to absorb all the spare capacity of both systems, this did not greatly matter, but it was another story during the years of the depression. With financial stability restored, work on the new lines was resumed and the secondary network was redefined in a new plan of 1922, much of it being brought into service between 1925 and 1930.

The years between the wars were marked by a spectacular growth of the suburban area immediately beyond the former fortifications, which were demolished by 1920, and by 1931 the population of the area was almost equal to that of the City itself. For the first time commuter traffic to and from the suburbs became an important factor in Paris transport and the immediate result was growing congestion at the outer terminal stations of the Métro and at the main line stations, particularly during the morning and evening peaks. In 1927 the City and the Département decided that the Métro should be extended into the suburbs and in 1929 the first tentative proposal for a regional express network of two lines was made. The original concept of the Métro as a purely urban system was clearly no longer appropriate and in October 1929 three agreements were made between the City, the Département, the CMP and the Nord-Sud company. Under these, the CMP resumed much of its former financial autonomy, 15 suburban extensions were to be constructed by the Département to be worked as part of the Métro and a separate fare system for the suburban area was to be created. The price exacted by the local authorities for this agreement was the fusion of the Nord-Sud with the CMP and this duly took place on 1 January 1930. In the following year, the lines of the former lost their unusual system of current collection and were converted to the CMP standard (although overhead pantograph operation was retained in Vaugirard depot yard until 1952). The two Nord-Sud lines A and B were renumbered 12 and 13 respectively, while the as-yet unbuilt line C (authorised back in 1912) became line 14.

Work on the suburban lines was begun immediately and the majority were brought into operation between 1934 and 1937, while two new urban lines, 11 and 14, were also opened. But in spite of the growth of the network, the 1930s were in general a period of declining traffic for the Métro. While some of the new extensions, such as that of line 1 to

Château de Vincennes, reported spectacular increases in passengers, there was clearly not room for the amount of competition then existing in Paris transport. As local authorities were clearly not willing to be saddled with responsibility for increasing fares or reducing services, the national government stepped in and on 12 November 1938 appointed a committee to co-ordinate transport in the Paris area.

The 1930s saw the retirement, at the age of 80 in 1932, of Fulgence Bienvenüe, followed by his death four years later. No other underground system has been so much the creation of one man, and the lasting success of the Métro owes much to his vision and his ability to plan beyond the next immediate step. To the Parisians generally, he was the 'Father of the Métro', while to his workers he was 'Father Métro', a strict but always just figure of authority. His services were recognised by both the Government, which ultimately awarded him the Grand Cross of the Legion of Honour, and by the City, from whom he received in 1924 a gold medal. His activities were by no means confined to the Métro; during the First World War, he re-organised the defences of Paris and also helped in the creation of the inland port at Gennevilliers. Even after his retirement, he continued to act as a consultant to the CMP and he had the pleasure of seeing the first suburban extensions opened for traffic. The success of the Métro during the Second World War was a tribute to his memory.

The outbreak of war and the subsequent political upheaval delayed the implementation of the policy of co-ordination. In fact, the first effect on the Métro was a contraction of the system. From 3 September 1939, the network was drastically reduced in size from 159km to 92.7km and only 85 stations were open. Lines 2, 6, 11 and 14 were closed in their entirety, as was the shuttle from Porte des Lilas to Pré-Saint-Gervais. Line 2 reopened on 27 June 1940, but some stations remained closed, while the line closed again from 23 to 28 July 1944. Line 6 reopened partially between Glacière and Étoile on 6 July 1940, the remainder nine days later. Line 11 reopened between Mairie des Lilas and Arts et Métiers on 5 February 1940 and to Châtelet on 9 July 1940; the whole line was closed again in 1944, when the occupying forces took it over to use as an underground factory, and it was not finally reopened until March 1945. Line 14 reopened earlier, on 30 September 1939 from Porte de Vanves to Duroc, and to Invalides on 9 July 1940.

Many individual Métro stations were closed for various periods during the war and even at the end of 1945, a total of 73 had still not been reopened to the public. Most of these reopened in the years that followed, but a small number remain closed to this day (q.v. Stations).

Once matters had settled down after the armistice in June 1940, the Vichy government resumed the previous policy, and in June 1941 passed a Law amalgamating the STCRP and the CMP with effect from New Year's Day 1942. In practice, the Métro took over the bus system, or at least such of it as was still extant. As the war progressed, the number of buses available for service decreased until there were only enough to maintain a very reduced service in the suburbs. For most of 1944 and 1945, there were no buses at all operating within the city of Paris. The Métro as a result had to cope with tremendous overcrowding. This increased after the war had ended, to the point where it became a major undertaking to travel during the rush hours, when it was nothing to wait ten minutes before one could even gain access to the platform, let alone get on a train. To help ease the situation, redundant staff were transferred from the road section and overhaul times for the rolling stock were reduced. Remarkably, the system coped without any major breakdown. Unfortunately, the memories of these years lingered on and made many people turn to private transport as soon as cars and petrol became available again. The Métro's success was turned against it. There was little physical damage to the Métro system during the war, although a few cars were destroyed by none-too-accurate Allied bombing of military targets. In the weeks immediately before the liberation of Paris, the whole system came to a standstill and reopening was a gradual process during the autumn of 1944. Thanks to a convenient, but largely-forgotten tunnel between the Préfecture of Police and Cité station (on line 4), resistance workers were able to use the tunnels to spread their activities around Paris while the occupying forces were still blockading the doorways of the same buildings, so even if somewhat passively, the Métro did play its part in the liberation of its city.

The provisional arrangement made in 1941 was not altogether satisfactory, as it was based on the legal position of the CMP and difficulties arose when the management of the bus system was grafted on to this. Nor, in the post-war political climate, was it any longer considered right for a private company to administer such a major public service and, as a temporary measure, a government administrator was placed in charge of the combined system from 1 January 1945. The administrative problems became particularly acute when it was realised that it would be necessary to borrow large sums of money to modernise the bus fleet. The bus services had by now been reorganised to act as feeders to the Métro instead of running in competition with it, but many of the vehicles were long past retirement. The government therefore set up another commission of inquiry in 1947 and this reported with commendable speed. Following its recommendations, two new bodies responsible for the capital's transport were created by a Law of 21 March 1948. The Office Régional des Transports Parisiens was intended to co-ordinate services (including those of the SNCF), to draw up plans for the future and to fix fares. The Régie Autonome des Transports Parisiens was responsible for the operation of the combined system. Apart from the replacement of the ORTP by the Syndicat des Transports Parisiens in 1959, the administrative structure created in 1948 has lasted to the present day, though in recent years the regional planning commission has played a considerable part in transport affairs.

For the Métro, the changes did not amount in practice to very much. In fact, if anything, the Métro was ushered into a period of stagnation. The autonomy of the RATP in its first years was largely fictional, since it was required to balance its budgets without being able to raise fares to take account of increased costs; permission to do so from the ORTP usually came far too late. Only by doing nothing in the way of modernisation was the RATP able to comply with the requirement in its first four years. The ruling was modified after 1952, when fares were frozen for some years for social reasons, but this still did not provide any funds for investment. Money was instead diverted by the central government to repair the ravages of the war years and to build up the main line railways and the road system. There was a general, though unspoken, assumption that public transport would quietly wither and that people would more and more take to the car as a means of getting around in the capital. And yet, despite public dissatisfaction with the standard of comfort offered by the Métro, it did not wither away. In the 1950s there was a phenomenal growth of population in both the inner and outer suburbs, accompanied by an equally rapid growth in car ownership. The type of traffic congestion formerly experienced only in the centre of Paris became commonplace in the suburbs, and by 1960 the Métro was carrying 1,200-million passengers per annum, an increase of 50% over the figure for 1938. A greater proportion was now carried in the peak hours and far more passengers came to the Métro from the suburban services of the SNCF.

In the light of this situation, the Government of the Fifth Republic began to allocate more money to investment in public transport in the Paris region. At first, most of this went to the Regional Express Métro for which some very grandiose schemes were drawn up, but in the mid-1960s, it was realised that the regional network was not going to be the solution to all the capital's transport problems. The original RER concept was part of a Traffic Master Plan which included hundreds of miles of motorways as well. It was realised soon after that this would result in choking the City of Paris and also that the RER would take far too long. Hence, to achieve speedier results, the attention was shifted to the Métro even though the developments were against a background of changing political balances. Coupled with this was an admission that reliance on conversion to operation by pneumatic-tyred trains as the only means of modernising the network would mean that the process would be protracted and would not be finished until about the year 2000, and therefore it would be better to consider using conventional solutions as well. The increased investment resulted in the development of new steel-tyred rolling stock, in the automation of many aspects of Métro operation, and in a great improvement in the equipment and decor of the stations. All this was an essential complement to the extensions which took place in the 1970s and which are still continuing, albeit at a slower rate. The modernisation of the Métro has also acted as a shop window for French industry, and has led to increased technical co-operation with, and orders from, many foreign rapid transit systems.

For the future, the Métro is seen as the main form of transport for the region of central Paris, and for the area lying between 5 and 10km from the centre. With its intricate network of lines, closely-spaced stations and frequent trains, it offers both substantial saving in time over road journeys and equalises the chances of access to the centre of the conurbation for car owners and non-car owners alike.

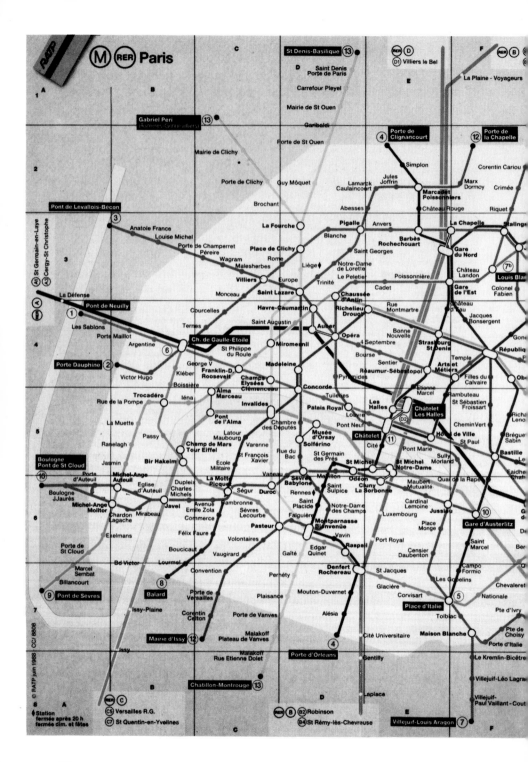

Paris métro/RER map

(7) La Courneuve-8 Mai 1945
Q
Fort d'Aubervilliers
ubervilliers-Pantin Chemins
e de la Villette
Bobigny-Pablo Picasso (5)
Bobigny-Pantin R. Queneau 2
Église de Pantin
Hoche
Porte de Pantin
Ourcq
umière
Pré-St Gervais
Danube (7b) 3
Botzaris
Buttes Chaumont
dain Télégraphe (11) Mairie des Lilas
Place des Fêtes (3b)
Pyrénées Saint Fargeau
eville Porte des Lilas
Couronnes Pelleport
Ménilmontant (3b) Gallieni
Saint Maur Gambetta (3) Porte de Bagnolet
Père Lachaise Mairie de Montreuil
Ambroise Philippe Auguste (9)
Croix de Chavaux
oltaire Alexandre Dumas Robespierre
Charonne Pte de Montreuil 5
ulets treuil Avron Maraîchers
lin (6) (2) Buzenval
Nation Porte de Vincennes
Vincennes (A) Boissy-St L.
(RER) Marne-la-V.
St Mandé Tourelle Bérault
Sully Diderot Picpus (1)
Bel Air Château de Vincennes
ntgallet
Daumesnil
Michel Bizot
Porte Dorée
Porte de Charenton 7
Liberté
d Massena Charenton-Ecoles
Gare Alfort-Ecole Vétérinaire
re rie Maisons-Alfort Stade
Ivry sur Seine Maisons-Alfort Les Juilliottes
(7) Créteil-l'Echat
Mairie d'Ivry Créteil Université 8
Vitry sur Seine
(RER)(C)
(C2) Massy-Palaiseau
(C4) Dourdan
(C6) St M. d'Etampes
Creteil-Prefecture (8)
H

Index des stations du Plan de Métro

CHAPTER 2
THE DEVELOPMENT OF THE NETWORK

Line 1

The premier line of the Métro – its original line – is line 1, which was opened on 19 July 1900 from Porte de Vincennes to Porte Maillot, running roughly on an east to west axis. At Porte de Vincennes, terminal arrangements were in the form of separate island platforms for arrival and departure, trains reversing beyond the station. At Porte Maillot, two separate island platforms were connected by a very sharply-curved single track loop, which avoided the need for trains to reverse. Apart from Bastille station, where it crosses over the Saint-Martin canal, the line operates in tunnel. The western end of Bastille station has the severest passenger curve on the whole of the Métro at 40m radius. Operation remained unchanged until an extension was opened beyond the city boundary from Porte de Vincennes to Château de Vincennes on 24 March 1934. The old terminal station at Porte de Vincennes was retained for the extension, but in later years the layout was altered to have one track in each direction. The original arrangement can be observed to this day, with the extra wide platforms. A westward extension was made to Pont de Neuilly on 29 April 1937, but prior to that, new platforms had been constructed at Porte Maillot and brought into use on 15 November 1936, in anticipation of the extension.

The old Classic stock was replaced by pneumatic-tyred trains, making their debut on 30 May 1963. The changeover in stock was completed by December 1964. Although line 11 had been converted to 'pneu' operation from 1957, line 1 was the first major Métro line to be so converted. This was far from simple, particularly as there was a tendency to drive the new stock like a Sprague train. Also, it was very hard for a Sprague train to keep up with the new stock. The present length of line 1 is 14.637km and in 1986 it was the Métro's third busiest line, carrying over 108 million passengers, slipping from second into third position, being overtaken by line 9.

Construction of an extension, 1.87km long, from Pont de Neuilly to La Défense has recently started, and should open in January 1992. On leaving Pont de Neuilly the line will rise sharply to street level and will run in the middle of autoroute A14, crossing the River Seine. Road traffic will be partly resited on the present pedestrian pavements and a new bridge will be provided for pedestrians. On the west side of the Pont de Neuilly the only intermediate station, Puteaux Corbevoie, will be situated, an island platform, partly in the open and partly in tunnel. The line will then run underground to La Défense, at which point provision has already been made for the new extension – this was done in 1970 when the station complex was first built for the RER.

The original terminus of Porte Maillot on line 1, which was abandoned in 1936, as seen in February 1988. The old station comprised two separate island platforms (one for arrival, one for departure) connected by a sharply-curved single track loop.

R.J. Greenaway

New platforms at Porte Maillot were built on the alignment of the extension to Pont de Neuilly and comprised two pairs of side platforms. The track on the left is used by (approaching) trains to Pont de Neuilly, while the one to the right is used for stabling trains. The Paris-bound pair of platforms is beyond the wall on the right. *R.J. Greenaway*

Line 2

Line 2 originally began as a shuttle from Étoile (now Charles de Gaulle-Étoile) to Porte Dauphine on 13 December 1900. The latter terminus is similar to the original line 1 terminus at Porte Maillot, the arrival and departure platforms being linked by a sharply-curved loop of 30m radius. The first part of the main portion of the line was opened from Étoile to Anvers on 7 October 1902, followed by the section onwards to Bagnolet (renamed Alexandre Dumas in 1970) on 31 January 1903. This latter section comprises 2.22km on viaduct, with four elevated stations (Barbès-Rochechouart, La Chapelle, Stalingrad and Jaurès), and crosses the main line exits from the Gare du Nord and Gare de l'Est, both almost at the end of the platforms. The last section onwards to Nation was completed on 2 April 1903 and the pattern of service has remained unchanged since then, though it should be mentioned that the line was known as 2 Nord (North) until 14 October 1907, from when it became line 2. The length of line is 12.316km, and operates wholly within the city boundary.

Line 3

Rather oddly, line 3 was not the next line to be opened (line 5 in fact got in before 3 and 4) and was inaugurated in stages, as follows:

Villiers to Père-Lachaise	19 October 1904
Père-Lachaise to Gambetta	25 January 1905
Villiers to Péreire	23 May 1910
Péreire to Porte de Champerret	15 February 1911

This line was the first to open after the Couronnes disaster (q.v. Rolling Stock) and incorporated improved safety features devised in the light of the experience gained from that. There was a system of emergency lighting for the tunnels, the wires for which were buried in the ballast, and the stations had improved emergency facilities. Villiers station was a terminus for just over five years and trains reversed in sidings away from the subsequent alignment to Champerret. These sidings beyond the station continue to be used for instructional purposes for train drivers, and hence two trains are based here. Line 3 was further extended at the eastern side of the city from Gambetta to Porte des Lilas on 27 November 1921. It was extended in the western suburbs, to Pont de Levallois on 24 September 1937.

A major upheaval in the line's history came in 1971 when the section from Gambetta to Porte des Lilas became a self-contained branch line (3bis) on 27 March in connection with the opening of an extension from Gambetta to a new transport interchange complex at Galliéni on 2 April 1971. This new line required the provision of 'through' platforms at Gambetta and these took in the platforms of nearby Martin Nadaud station, which effectively closed. This had been, at 0.23km, the shortest distance between any pair of stations on the Métro. The island platform at Gambetta in the Paris direction became the terminal platform for line 3bis, while the other platforms were demolished. The careful observer will notice (just) the remains of the old tiled walls of the station, on leaving Gambetta heading towards Galliéni. Line connections continue to exist at Gambetta between the branch and the main line and a maximum of 13 trains from line 3 are stabled at night at Porte des Lilas, running empty from Gambetta.

Line 3 was the first to receive modern steel-wheel trains from late-1967, but 3bis continued to operate the old Classic stock until 2 July 1981. The main line is now 11.684km long and the branch 1.289km – all of it underground.

Line 4

The unexpected difficulties found in the construction of a tunnel under the River Seine meant that line 4 was, unusually, originally opened as two disconnected pieces. The northern section between Porte de Clignancourt and Châtelet was the first to open on 21 April 1908, while the southern section between Porte d'Orléans and Raspail followed on 30 October 1909. The two sections were finally connected on 9 January 1910 and the line has not been extended since then, a 1928 proposal for an extension from the southern terminus to Carrefour de la Vache Noire not having been pursued. However, a 330m long deviation of the line was made from 3 October 1977 in connection with a new station at Les Halles, 30m to the east, to make interchange with the enormous RER complex easier.

Conversion to pneumatic-tyred trains took place between October 1966 and July 1967. This line, 10.598km long and all underground, is presently the busiest on the Métro, carrying over 133 million passengers in 1986. This number has not diminished to any great degree with the opening of new sections of the RER.

Saint Fargeau station on line 3bis is very much an original Métro station, and typical of how most used to be, with tiled names, wooden bench seats and decorative tiled advertisement surrounds.
R.J. Greenaway

Château d'Eau station on line 4, seen in March 1988, is typical of a station built by the cut-and-cover method, instantly recognisable by the roof-level cross girders and the straight-sided platform tiled walls. *John Thomason*

Lines 5 and 6

The second Métro line to be opened was what is now line 6, from Étoile to Trocadéro on 2 October 1900. This line was at first known as line 2 Sud (South) and was extended from Trocadéro to Passy on 6 November 1903 and on to Place d'Italie on 24 April 1906. There it was soon joined by line 5, whose first section from Place d'Italie to Gare d'Orléans (now Gare d'Austerlitz) was opened on 2 June of the same year. Line 5 had been originally intended to run from the Gare de l'Est to the Pont d'Austerlitz via the Gare de Lyon, but it soon became obvious that this would involve an impossibly steep gradient from the latter station up to the viaduct over the River Seine, and the line as built was diverted to the west to run via Quai de la Rapée (at that date known as Place Mazas and renamed Pont d'Austerlitz from 1907 to 1916), a connection being provided to the Gare de Lyon. It was then decided that line 5 should incorporate the section on to Place d'Italie originally intended to have been part of line 2 Sud, and this was in fact the first portion to be opened. Line 5 was extended to Place Mazas on 14 July 1906, from which date a connecting shuttle service was provided to Gare de Lyon. From 1 August 1906 this was replaced by a through service with trains having to reverse at Place Mazas, but when a northbound extension to Lancry (now Jacques Bonsergent) was opened on 17 December 1906, the service to Gare de Lyon was abandoned, leaving this station rather isolated on line 1 until the RER was built some seventy years later. The abandoned section served, between 1937 and 1967, as the 'finance line', where a motor car collected cash from stations to be taken to Gare de Lyon. It still serves to transfer rolling stock between lines 1 and 5, and also is used for instructional purposes for train drivers, where two trains are based.

The use of Place d'Italie as a terminus for lines 2 Sud and 5 was inconvenient for both operating staff and passengers and on 14 October 1907 the lines were amalgamated under the latter number. From the same date, line 2 Nord became line 2. A northward extension to the Gare du Nord followed on 15 November 1907, after which the service remained unchanged for many years, although from 17 May to 6 December 1931, during the period of the Colonial Exhibition, it was curtailed to run from Place d'Italie to Gare du Nord.

The CMP was not particularly enthusiastic about line 6 in the early days, as it did not promise to generate much traffic and, though the infrastructure was completed by the City from Place d'Italie through to Nation in 1906, the Company took refuge in a clause in the original agreement which said that lines should be opened in the order they were listed therein and consequently they did not begin to operate line 6 until after the first section of line 4 had been placed in service. The actual opening date was 1 March 1909. The line was briefly extended to Étoile in 1931 in place of line 5 (q.v. above).

An extension of line 5 from Gare du Nord to Eglise de Pantin was under construction in 1939 but the opening was delayed by the outbreak of the Second World War and it was not until 6 October 1942 that new platforms were opened at Gare du Nord on the alignment of the extension. The extension itself was brought into operation on 12 October 1942. As line 5 would then have become too long for reasonable operation, it was, from the same date, curtailed to terminate at Place d'Italie. The section between Place d'Italie and Étoile was transferred to line 6, also on 12 October 1942, and this line then described a southern arc of the City. The former line 5 terminus at Gare du Nord is used for train driver instruction with three trains being based there for such duties.

Gare d'Austerlitz on line 5 is situated high above and in the roof of the SNCF station. In 1985 the Métro station was updated with new signs and seats, and improved lighting. The train on the right-hand track is heading away from the camera for the northern terminus of Bobigny.
R.J. Greenaway

A train of MF67F stock approaches Gare d'Austerlitz on line 5, having crossed the River Seine on the impressive Austerlitz bridge, seen in the background. The conventional track arrangement can be observed in the picture, with the 750V dc current rail higher than the running rails, and offset to one side between them is the track ATO equipment. The Paris Métro operates with right-hand running throughout the network. *Brian Hardy*

Much of line 6 is in the open air – in stark contrast to other early Métro lines. Over 6km of the 13.624km route length is on viaduct. Line 5 is mostly in the open from north of Campo-Formio to just beyond Quai de la Rapée, and this section is most interesting to the enthusiast. Climbing onto an elevated structure, the station of Gare d'Austerlitz is located in the roof of the SNCF station. The line then crosses the River Seine on the Austerlitz bridge before curving and descending sharply into tunnel, in which the connection to and from Gare de Lyon on line 1 is situated, and then rising again to the surface at Quai de la Rapée. Not surprisingly, this section has earned the title of 'the toboggan'. On leaving Quai de la Rapée station the line immediately crosses the Saint Martin canal and then continues underground.

Line 6 was converted for pneumatic-tyred trains between October 1972 and May 1974. In comparison to other 'pneu' conversions, line 6 was undertaken mainly for environmental reasons, to reduce noise on the open sections of the line. The rolling stock was changed over from July 1974. It was originally intended that the conversion of line 2 would similarly follow and that the two lines would be linked, making one large circular service, but this plan has now been shelved.

After over forty years of unchanged operation, line 5 was extended in 1985, from Eglise de Pantin to Bobigny - Pablo Picasso, opening on 25 April, with one intermediate station named Bobigny Pantin - Raymond Queneau. Among the problems encountered with the construction of this extension was the severe flooding on 6 June 1982 which filled, and subsequently burst through, the new workings, and onto the existing Métro system at Eglise de Pantin. Here, 18 trains that were stabled were severely damaged by the immense torrent of water, all of which had to receive major workshop attention. On the new extension, the route crosses the Paris-Strasbourg main line and the Ourcq canal, both underground. Part of the line, between Bobigny Pantin and Bobigny-Pablo Picasso, is in the open and stabling sidings were built on the north side of the line, which has accommodation for over two-thirds of the rolling stock for line 5. A maintenance depot has also been built, which opened in April 1988. The distance between these two stations, at 2.43km, is now the longest interstation section on the Métro network. The route length of line 5 is 14.629km.

For the short distance between Passy and Bir-Hakeim, line 6 crosses the Seine on a viaduct and passes near the Eiffel Tower. The Métro viaduct itself sits on top of a road bridge. *R.J. Greenaway*

Below left A most unusual station on the Métro is Passy on line 6, which was the terminus of line 2 Sud between 1903 and 1906. It is unusual in that it is built partly in tunnel, partly on ground level (foreground) and on viaduct (farthest from the camera). A train of MP73 stock arrives, heading for Charles de Gaulle-Étoile. The close spacing of Métro stations can be appreciated here, with Bir-Hakeim easily seen in the background. *R.J. Greenaway*

Below right The majority of the elevated stations on line 6 comprise an all-over glass roof, as seen here at La Motte Picquet. The next station east, Cambronne, can be observed in the background. *Brian Hardy*

Bottom right A ground-level view of a typical elevated station on line 6 – Bir-Hakeim – with a train of MP73 stock arriving. *R.J. Greenaway*

Line 7

The history of line 7 is perhaps the most complex of any Métro line. It was originally intended that it should run from Opéra to a terminus in the north-east of the City, but the municipal authorities were unable to decide on the exact location of this terminus and in the end it was arranged that it should in fact take the form of a large loop, which would incorporate all of the proposed stations. It was later decided to add a branch to Porte de la Villette. The presence of old underground quarry workings under the Buttes-Chaumont caused problems in the construction of the line in that area and the first section to be opened was in fact from Opéra to Porte de la Villette on 5 November 1910. The line from Louis Blanc to Pré-Saint-Gervais was added on 18 January 1911. This was the first 'branch' of the Métro in the true sense and trains ran in an anti-clockwise direction round the loop. The outbreak of the First World War in 1914 delayed the opening of an extension from Opéra to Palais-Royal until 1 July 1916, although the work on the stations had not quite been finished even then. Extensions onwards to Pont Marie followed on 16 April 1926, to Sully Morland on 3 June 1930 and to Place Monge on 26 April 1931. The line thence south to Porte de Choisy had already been opened for traffic on 7 March 1930 and had been worked temporarily on an extension of line 10. It now assumed its intended role as part of line 7 and was extended to Porte d'Ivry, also on 26 April 1931. One of the few extensions to the Métro in the immediate post-war period took line 7 further south from Porte d'Ivry to Mairie d'Ivry on 1 May 1946.

At the northern end of line 7, the branch line to Pré-Saint-Gervais became a self-contained service as line 7bis from 3 December 1967, to allow a more frequent service to operate to Porte de la Villette. Whilst the main line received new rolling stock from June 1971, the branch 7bis continued to operate Classic stock until July 1980.

Although one of the Métro's longer lines for many years, a number of extensions have been made to line 7. In the north, a two-station extension from Porte de la Villette to Fort d'Aubervilliers was made on 4 October 1979. At the southern end the first stage of a new branch reached Le Kremlin-Bicêtre on 10 December 1982 and although it was the intention to serve each branch with alternate trains, it was soon found necessary to operate a pattern in the evening peaks so that Mairie d'Ivry had two trains to Le Kremlin-Bicêtre's one, because of the uneven traffic flows. This situation was rectified when the ultimate southern terminus of Villejuif-Louis Aragon was reached on 28 February 1985. Trains were then able to serve the two southern branches alternately, and indeed, both have identical running times from end to end. The final extension to line 7 was opened to the public on 6 May 1987, when the northern terminus was extended one station to La Courneuve – 8 Mai 1945. With a total route length of 22.8km, line 7 is now the longest of all Métro lines and operates the most trains in service (65) at peak times. Both line 7 and branch line 7bis (3.066km) are wholly underground.

Lines 8, 9 and 10

The history of these three lines is also rather complex, and as they were planned and, to a certain extent, built together, they will be dealt with as a group.

Line 8 was mentioned in the first plans, but only as a line which should be constructed at a later date. It was finally agreed in 1903 that it should be built from the Opéra to Auteuil, with a branch to Porte de Sèvres (now Place Balard). However, before any work was done, the line became merged in a much grander scheme. In 1907 the municipal authorities adopted a plan for an additional network, to follow the construction of the main system. This plan included the first part of line 9 and also an inner circle, to run from Invalides to Invalides via the Boulevard Saint Germain, Bastille, République and Opéra. Between République and Invalides this line would share the tracks of line 8 to which line 9 might also be added. It was also planned that line 8 would include a connection to line 9 at the southern end to allow trains on both lines to serve both termini. It was all a very far cry from the lines that were already in operation, with their simple end-to-end services. Fortunately, the City and the CMP later had second thoughts – perhaps someone came to London and had a close look at the complex workings of the Inner Circle! – and the grand design was never put into operation. However, it did influence both the course of the lines under discussion and the layout of the tracks in various places, such as in the vicinity of Invalides station, and it is therefore important to bear in mind what the original plans were.

Probably THE most interesting and unusual station on the Métro can be seen at Mirabeau on line 10 (originally line 8 until 1937), where there is only one platform, in the Paris direction. Trains to Porte d'Auteuil and Boulogne emerge from the tunnel after crossing under the River Seine and pass through the station on a steep uphill gradient.   *John Thomason*

A train of MF77 stock pauses for passengers at Lourmel on line 8. The overhead wires to provide emergency lighting on old stock trains and power to works trains are still in situ, although they have been disused since September 1987. This is another example of an almost original Métro station although opened in 1937.
R.J. Greenaway

On the few Métro lines which have branches or short workings, (lines 7, 8, 10 and 13) the choice of destination is shown by illuminating blue or yellow lights (in the case of line 10, referring to Boulogne or Porte d'Auteuil respectively) both inside and outside the trains. The colour codes, where applicable, are used also on destination blinds, and destination indicators on stations.
R.J. Greenaway

19

Line 8 was inaugurated on 13 July 1913 when the section from Opéra to Beaugrenelle (named Charles Michels since 1945) was opened to traffic. It was extended to Porte d'Auteuil in the form of an anti-clockwise loop on 30 September of the same year. The eastern end was extended from Opéra to Richelieu-Drouot on 30 June 1928 and further to Porte de Charenton on 5 May 1931 in time to serve the Colonial Exhibition of that year, held in what is now called the Musée des Arts Africains et Océaniens at Porte Dorée. In 1937 there was a major re-arrangement of the south-western end of the line, which was diverted at La Motte-Picquet and extended to Balard, its previous operation to Auteuil being taken over by line 10. A south-eastern extension was opened on 5 October 1942 from Porte de Charenton to Charenton-Ecoles.

After a long period of stagnation on the Métro generally, line 8 was the first of several lines to be extended in the 1970s. Four separate stages took the line from Charenton-Ecoles to Créteil-Préfecture, as follows:

Charenton-Ecoles to Maisons-Alfort-Stade	19 September 1970
Maisons-Alfort-Stade to Maisons-Alfort-les Juilliottes	27 April 1972
Maisons-Alfort-les Juilliottes to Créteil-l'Echat	26 September 1973
Créteil-l'Echat to Créteil-Préfecture	10 September 1974

This extension differed from all previous extensions in that the distance between stations was on average much greater (1km as against 0.5km) and also because for the first time a supplementary fare was levied for travel on it as proposed in the 1929 plans. Supplementary fares have, however, since 1 November 1982, been discontinued. The open-air section to Créteil is, unusually, built in the central reservation of a motorway and the space for three tracks has been provided throughout. On only some of the route from Maisons-Alfort-les Juilliottes to Créteil-Préfecture has a third track actually been provided. The intention is to operate semi-fast working if desired at a later date, but for the moment, the third (western) track is used for stabling trains. Line 8 is 22.05km long.

Line 9 was originally seen as a branch of what was then line 2 Sud from Trocadéro to Porte de Saint-Cloud. In 1907, however, it was decided that it should be extended inwards to Opéra as an independent line. Then for a brief period it was envisaged that it would be worked as a branch of the proposed inner circle. Finally, it was evident that this would overload the circle and the line was constructed on its own. The exact location of the terminal sidings at Porte de Saint-Cloud caused problems and construction was delayed not only by the outbreak of war, but also by a collapse of the workings at Place de l'Alma on 8 November 1915 and by the post-war financial troubles of the CMP. The first section, from Exelmans to Trocadéro, was therefore not opened to the public until 8 November 1922. It was extended inwards to Saint-Augustin on 27 May 1923, to Chaussée d'Antin on 3 June 1923 and outwards to Porte de Saint-Cloud from Exelmans on 29 September of the same year. When the last part of the line was opened, it was planned that for special events at the Parc des Princes stadium, alternate trains would be diverted south of Jasmin on to what was then line 8 (now line 10) via the Auteuil loop at a special station at Porte Molitor. This island platform station was completed at track level but no connection had been made to street level when the project was abandoned, as it had been decided to keep lines 8 and 9 quite separate. From Porte Molitor trains would have returned to line 9 via a large loop near Porte de Saint-Cloud. The section of line concerned is now used for stabling trains from line 9, being part of a maze of tunnels in the area. Another proposal for line 9 which was not carried out was for a branch line from Saint-Augustin to Place des Ternes on line 2. At the former, the 'wide' platform in the eastbound direction is a relic of these plans, now used, on occasions, for exhibition purposes.

In the inner area, lines 8 and 9 were extended together, but on separate tracks, to Richelieu-Drouot on 30 June 1928, this section being originally planned as part of the inner circle. From there, tunnels for both lines, with separate tracks, were constructed onwards to République, not without considerable opposition from property owners along the line of the Grandes Boulevards, and line 9 was extended to Porte de Montreuil on 10 December 1933. The south-western terminus became Pont de Sèvres on 3 February 1934 (in fact the very first Métro extension beyond the City boundary) and the final extension in the east to Mairie de Montreuil followed on 14 October 1937.

The total length of line 9, at 19.565km, has been unchanged since 1937 and all of it operates underground. Line 9 was the last of all to operate the old Classic stock, the last trains running on 16 April 1983.

A view of the never-opened station at Porte Molitor, used for storing materials and stabling trains from line 10.
An articulated train of MA52 stock is seen on the right.   *R.J. Greenaway*

When construction work began on line 10 in 1913, it was still envisaged that this line would ultimately form part of the proposed inner circle and it was not until 1922, by which time a large junction layout had been constructed at Invalides, that it was decided that it should instead be confined to the Left Bank of the Seine. It was opened from Invalides to Croix Rouge (the latter station, situated between Sèvres-Babylone and Mabillon, is now closed) on 30 December 1923 and traffic levels were at first derisory, since their two termini were not very far apart and the intermediate stations served no very recognisable flow of passengers. It was extended one station to Mabillon on 10 March 1925 and on to Odéon on 14 February 1926. To work line 10 more economically, a series of motor coaches with driving cabs at both ends, capable of running as single units, was placed into service in 1925.

Line 10 was extended briefly to Place d'Italie on 15 February 1930 and to Porte de Choisy on 7 March 1931. These extensions brought it an increased but unbalanced traffic. When line 7 reached the Left Bank, it assumed operation of the new section to Porte de Choisy and line 10 was instead diverted to terminate at Jussieu, reached on 26 April 1931.

With another fairly drastic re-arrangement, carried out between 26 and 29 July 1937, line 10 was extended at Duroc over a newly-built section of track to La Motte-Picquet, then by the tracks of the former line 8 to Porte d'Auteuil. The section northwards to Invalides was handed over to a new line 14. At the eastern end, line 10 was extended from Jussieu to Gare d'Austerlitz on 12 July 1939, a distance of 1.03km, making this the longest distance between two stations until the extensions of the 1970s. Nevertheless, this is still the longest distance on the Métro within the City boundary.

Line 10 was then to remain unaltered until the opening of a western extension to Boulogne - Jean Jaurès on 3 October 1980, and to Boulogne - Pont de Saint-Cloud on 2 October 1981. With the exception of the evening service, alternate trains still terminate at Porte d'Auteuil, giving the northern section of the one-way loop a through service into Paris. In the evenings, all trains work through to Boulogne and passengers for Paris have first to travel to Boulogne - Jean Jaurès and change trains there; cross-platform interchange is timetabled. All of line 10 operates underground, and is 11.708km long.

Line 11

Compared with other lines, the history of line 11 is simplicity itself. It was originally planned in 1922 and opened from Châtelet to Porte des Lilas on 28 April 1935 and one station further on to Mairie des Lilas on 17 February 1937. As it was built much later than the other lines, line 11 usually had to pass under these when it crossed them, and the sharp curves and gradients thus created made it an ideal proving ground for the operation of pneumatic-tyred trains, which went into service from 8 November 1956. The first essays of Automatic Train Operation in revenue service were also made on line 11 from September 1967 and following its success, the conversion of all its trains was completed by June 1969, the first line on the Métro to be so operated.

At a modest 6.287km in length, line 11 takes just 15 minutes from one end to the other – all underground.

Line 12

Line 12 was originally line A of the Nord-Sud company and was planned as a tube from Montmartre to Montparnasse. A few preliminary soundings showed that this would be an impossible undertaking and when construction actually began in 1907, it was as a conventional underground Métro. The workings ran into the same difficulties with abandoned quarry workings as were found on line 7 of the CMP and they were further held up by a series of strikes and by the disasterous floods of January 1910. There was something of a race with the CMP who were then completing the equipping of line 7 and in the end, both lines were opened on the same day – 5 November 1910. The first section open to traffic was from Porte de Versailles to Notre-Dame-de-Lorette, and extensions northwards brought the line to Pigalle on 8 April 1911, Jules Joffrin on 31 October 1912, and Porte de la Chapelle on 23 August 1916. This last extension was opened despite a shortage of rolling stock, as the firm that was then building some additional trains was in that part of Northern France then occupied by the German army. No further extensions were made to line 12 while the Nord-Sud retained its independence. In fact, the only extension to be made in CMP days was from Porte de Versailles to Mairie d'Issy on 24 March 1934, since when the operation of line 12 has not changed. The complete 13.888km of line 12 is in tunnel.

Lines 13 and 14

The second and, as events turned out, final Nord-Sud line was line 13 (line B), opened from Saint-Lazare to Porte de Saint-Ouen on 26 February 1911, followed on 20 January 1912 by a branch from La Fourche to Porte de Clichy, trains serving each destination alternately. The line served densely populated working class districts and soon built up a good level of traffic. However, there was not much demand for first class travel and in due course the first class trailer cars were converted to composite cars, in order to increase the second class accommodation, the first such vehicles on either system.

The main line was extended from Porte de Saint-Ouen to Carrefour Pleyel on 30 June 1952, one of only two such short extensions to the Métro in the early-post war period, until the 'rebirth' of the Métro from the 1970s.

Line 14 was originally planned as line C of the Nord-Sud company, but it was not built as such. Construction did not begin until 1934 and line 14 came into service with the opening of the section from Porte de Vanves to Avenue du Maine (renamed Bienvenüe in 1942) on 21 January 1937. Further new tunnels from the latter station to Duroc were opened on 27 July 1937, on which date the section of line 10 from Duroc to Invalides was handed over to the new line 14. The terminal working arrangements at Invalides required departing trains to traverse a large loop, before taking up normal running at the first station south – Varenne.

One of the early plans for the RER envisaged a line linking the Gare Montparnasse with Saint-Lazare, but it was soon realised that such a link could be provided at a fraction of the cost by connecting lines 13 and 14, and operating them as a combined through service. This would relieve congestion at Saint-Lazare, which was then (and has recently reverted to being) the busiest Métro station, and would improve capacity on line 13 from there to the two northern branches. In addition, the expanding business centres between there and Montparnasse justified this new extension, but also allowed a 25–30% easing on line 12 between these two points.

At the same time that lines 13 and 14 were linked in central Paris, the southern end of what was line 14 was extended south from Porte de Vanves to Châtillon-Montrouge, where at the latter, a train of MF77 stock is seen arriving.

R.J. Greenaway

Both northern branches of line 13 have been extended, that beyond Porte de Clichy to Gabriel Péri in May 1980. An MF77 train is seen at the intermediate station of Mairie de Clichy, recognisable as being built by the cut and cover method by its rectangular 'box' shape. A sound baffle can be seen dividing the two tracks.

R.J. Greenaway

The route taken by the line 13–14 link from Saint-Lazare was via Miromesnil, at which location the new station was built under and at right angles to that on line 9, thence to Champs-Élysées-Clemenceau (providing interchange with line 1) and to Invalides, at which station trains no longer had to traverse a large loop when travelling south.

The connection between lines 13 and 14 was actually achieved in three stages,

Saint-Lazare to Miromesnil	27 June 1973
Miromesnil to Champs-Élysées-Clémenceau	18 February 1975
Champs-Élysées-Clémenceau to Invalides	9 November 1976

When the last section was opened, the complete line became one line 13.

Not only were lines 13 and 14 joined in the centre of Paris, but extensions were being made at both northern and southern ends into the suburbs. Previously, on 20 May 1976, the northern end of the main line was extended from Carrefour Pleyel to Saint-Denis-Basilique, and on the date that lines 13 and 14 merged, a southern extension was opened from Porte de Vanves to Châtillon-Montrouge, the last two stations on this new section being in the open air.

Thus, by the construction of a mere 7km of new Métro line, a regional link was created, which filled several awkward gaps in the existing network and provided connections with ten other Métro lines. In 1978 line 13 was the recipient of the new MF77 trains, the line being completely worked by this stock in late-1979.

The northern branch was extended from Porte de Clichy to Gabriel Péri (Asnières-Gennevilliers) on 9 May 1980, and a crossing of the River Seine is made in the open on viaduct between Mairie de Clichy and the terminus.

There are two separate operating patterns on line 13. In peak hours, the service ratio is two trains to Saint-Denis and one to Gabriel Péri, while at all other times, each destination is served alternately. The distances on line 13 from Châtillon-Montrouge to the north end terminal stations are 16.854km (Saint-Denis) and 14.77km (Gabriel Péri).

The Shuttle (Navette)

Apart from the Quai de la Rapée to Gare de Lyon section of line 5, which saw only five months of passenger service in the autumn of 1906, there is only one section of the Métro which has been closed to passengers. This is a section of line, 767m long, on which a shuttle service was formerly operated between Porte des Lilas and Pré-Saint-Gervais. The original intention in 1907 was to extend line 3 in the outward direction from Gambetta to Pré-Saint-Gervais as line 3ter and to provide a connection for the opposite direction from line 7 at Place des Fêtes, but by the time the line was actually completed in 1920, the CMP had given up this idea and had decided to operate the section Porte des Lilas to Pré-Saint-Gervais simply as a shuttle service. It was actually opened as La Navette (the shuttle) on 27 November 1921, at the same date as line 3 was extended from Gambetta to Porte des Lilas. A single train of two motor coaches was sufficient for the meagre traffic, and even this was later replaced by a double-ended single motor coach.

With the outbreak of the Second World War, the shuttle was closed from 3 September 1939. The line was later used for experiments with pneumatic tyred trains from 1951 and in the following year, beginning on 13 April, the public were allowed to use the single 'pneu' motor coach as it shuttled to and fro. However, there was never any intention to restore a regular service as such and anyway passengers were only carried between the hours of 13.30 and 19.30. No service was provided when the coach was off for maintenance, which took place on a storage track at Porte des Lilas. Experiments with Automatic Train Operation were also carried out on this line from 1951 onwards. There was little traffic apart from sightseers and school children and the line was closed again when trials came to to an end on 31 May 1956. Since that date the line has been used mainly for driver training, where one train of 'pneu' stock has been located at Porte des Lilas in the former shuttle platform since 1981. Between there and Pré-Saint-Gervais the line is being used (in 1988) for experiments in 'no-person-operation' – Automobilisation Integrale du Movement des Trains (AIMT). The other platform (which has never been used by passengers) is used for filming purposes. Between Porte des Lilas and Place des Fêtes, the platform of an intermediate station at Haxo was completed on the southern track only, but (like that at Porte Molitor between lines 9 and 10) it was not connected to the street. This southern track is used to stable trains from line 3, which run empty to and from Gambetta.

Proposed Extensions

In 1973, after the completion of the extension to line 3, and while the extensions of lines 8 and 13 were proceeding, an overall plan for future extensions to the Métro was drawn up which, in 1976, was incorporated into the Government's plans for urban development in the Île-de-France Region. These extensions were intended to satisfy four objectives:

- Improvement in the accessibility of Paris to the inhabitants of the inner suburbs, and, by feeder bus routes to those of the outer suburbs,
- Increasing mobility for those who were not car owners, thus lessening social inequalities,
- Reduction in traffic congestion and its associated nuisances, and
- Improvement in the flow of traffic.

In all, twelve extensions were planned, which would effectively double the coverage of the inner suburbs by the Métro. Those opened so far or under construction have already been covered under the appropriate lines, while others proposed are as follows:

Line 4 – From Porte d'Orléans to Montrouge and Bagneux,
Line 8 – From Créteil-Préfecture to Parc Régional,
Line 9 – From Mairie de Montreuil to Rosny-sous-Bois,
Line 11 – From Mairie des Lilas to Romainville,
Line 13 – From Saint-Denis to Université du Nord: Gabriel Péri (Asnières-Gennevilliers) to a station known as Asnières-Gennevilliers III: Châtillon-Montrouge to Châtillon II.

The actual realisation of all these extensions depends on various criteria, quite apart from cost. Population and the number of jobs in an area, socio-economic returns, the effect on other forms of transport and on urban development generally are all taken into account by the Regional Council when deciding the order of priority.

Given current restrictions on capital expenditure, the pressing need to provide relief for RER line A and the growing interest in France in tramways and light rapid transit, it is a matter of speculation if and when the above proposed extensions will be put into effect.

However, one new Métro line which may become a reality, subject to approval and funding being available, will be from Maison Blanche to Saint-Lazare, a distance of 12.2km and running via Gare de Lyon, République, Château Landon, Gare du Nord and Chaussée d'Antin. This will partly relieve the present overcrowding problems on RER line A, being capable of carrying 35,000 passengers an hour. Being an entirely new line, it is planned that it will be a 'pneu' line but operating at higher speeds than could hitherto be achieved. It will provide interchange with eleven Métro lines and all four RER lines. A further extension under consideration beyond Saint-Lazare could take this new line on to Porte Maillot via Ternes. If approval is given in 1988, it is anticipated that the first section, between Gare de Lyon and Saint-Lazare, could be operational by 1995.

The only extension to the Métro actually under construction at present is that on line 1 from Pont de Neuilly to La Défense, where on 19 February 1988 this picture was taken. On leaving the present terminus at Pont de Neuilly the line will rise to the surface and cross this bridge in the middle of the autoroute A14 (left). The road is in the earliest stages of widening (right) and a new bridge is being built for pedestrians to the right of that
R.J. Greenaway

Unfulfilled Plans

By comparison with other cities, Paris appears to have an extremely dense network of lines in the inner area, but in fact not all the lines originally planned were built, and it may be useful to summarise these here.

Leaving aside early proposals, the first line which did not pass beyond the planning stage was one mentioned as line G in the 1898 agreement to run along the Left Bank of the Seine from Place Valhubert to Quai de Conti. This was in fact the route taken by the Orléans Railway for its 1900 extension to the Gare d'Orsay and perhaps it was simply intended to block this piece of main line expansionism. At all events, it soon vanished from all plans for the Métro.

Both line 4 and line 7 were intended to cross the River Seine much further to the west than their present-day route, but in each case the existence of large numbers of historic buildings on each bank obliged the City to construct rather tortuous deviations, though line 4 thus gained access to some useful sources of additional traffic, as at Châtelet.

The original plans for the additional network envisaged a branch of line 9 from Saint-Augustin to Place des Ternes, as well as the inner circle (q.v. above). Line 4 was also to have had a peripheral extension from Porte d'Orléans to Porte de Gentilly; when the fortifications of Paris were being taken down in 1920, it was proposed to build this extension at ground level and to prolong it to Porte d'Italie as a separate line 12. In 1931, when the ex-Nord-Sud line A took the number 12, the proposed line then received the number 15 in the plans, but it was becoming apparent that it would be unlikely to generate much traffic, and shortly afterwards it disappeared into oblivion.

Of the 15 extensions into the suburbs planned in 1930, only eleven were actually built, and even the last of these were not completed until 1952. Two more, the northern extensions of lines 7 and 13, have been carried out in recent years, but extensions southwards of line 4 to Carrefour de la Vache Noire and northwards of line 12 from Porte de la Chapelle to Eglise Saint-Denis were dropped from the plans after 1945. The link to Eglise de Pantin was in fact provided by line 5, not by a branch of line 7 as first suggested, and line 11 stopped at Mairie des Lilas, one station short of its intended terminus at Fort de Noisy.

Finally, two plans of the late-1960s now seem unlikely to be realised. The first was to extend line 7bis via the Gare du Nord to Saint-Lazare and link it with the (then) Porte de Clichy branch of line 13. The other plan was to take line 5 on at its southern terminus end to Cité Universitaire, to provide interchange with what was then the Ligne de Sceaux (now RER line B) and to serve a district whose links with central Paris were rather poor. The extension of RER line B from its isolated terminus at Luxembourg to Châtelet-les-Halles and Gare du Nord has removed the need for this facility and the lack of finance has probably put paid to the former plan. At the same time, two route deviations were also canvassed; one would have taken line 2 to Gare du Nord, thus saving many passengers the trouble of changing one station or walking the long corridors between La Chapelle and Gare due Nord, and the other would have diverted line 5 to avoid the famous 'toboggan' at Quai de la Rapée and serve instead Gare de Lyon as in the original plans. Construction of the works for the new RER lines has probably made these proposed alterations impossible, and has in any case removed much of the need for them.

CHAPTER 3
MÉTRO OPERATIONS

Signalling

As far as can be ascertained, line 1 was opened for traffic without the protection of signals of any kind. As there were only ten trains operating on a ten or twelve minute headway, a time interval system apparently sufficed. However, on 20 September 1900, a new timetable doubled the service and it seems that this coincided with the adoption of a full system of signalling.

The first system to be adopted was the Hall block system, a mechanical one in which the signals were set by the passage of trains. The leading wheel of the first coach depressed a treadle at the side of the track and this in turn activated the signal arm, causing a disc to move and change the signal to caution (green). It also changed the last signal but one to clear (white). A green signal could be passed at reduced speed. Not surprisingly, this was open to abuse and on 19 October 1900 there was a rear-end collision between Champs-Élysées and Concorde, when a train set back and was run into by the following one, which was running under clear signals. Fortunately, there was no serious injury to passengers or crew. The green signal indications were then replaced by red and it was forbidden to pass a red signal except on written order, and then at only 10 km/hour. When line 2 (Nord) was opened, the system was modified further and the signals remained normally at red, clearing to white only immediately in front of a train and so avoiding any confusion with street lamps on the overhead section. The elevated part of line 2 Sud used semaphore signals similar to those of the main line railways. With careful maintenance, the Hall system worked quite well, but the trackside treadles were very easily put out of alignment and its use was not further extended after the opening of line 3.

Its successor was known as the Métro automatic block system. In this, a bar about five metres long was placed parallel to the running rails, on the opposite side of the track to the third rail. When energised by contact with the collector shoe of a passing train, the bar transmitted an electrical impulse, changing the signal to clear or danger as required. The system was installed on lines 4 to 8 as they were opened and between 1914 and 1918 replaced the Hall signalling on lines 1, 2 (Nord and Sud) and 3.

The Nord-Sud company, ever independent, made use of an entirely different system based on track circuits and relays. The entry of a train into a section caused a short circuit and cut off current from the relays, putting the signal at danger behind the train. It remained so until the train had cleared the next section ahead. At stations, three aspect signals were used, a green distant allowing entry to the station at reduced speed as soon as the preceding train had left. At the exits from stations there were two red indications and one white, one red being extinguished to allow departure when the train ahead had cleared the first section. The three aspect signals were ultimately introduced on the CMP, but the track circuits were given up in 1932, two years after the Nord-Sud was taken over.

From 1921, the CMP had in fact adopted a very similar system, but using alternating current for the track circuits rather than direct current. Unlike both the previous Métro block and the Nord-Sud systems, signals were normally clear, and changed to danger only with the passage of a train. The system was first used on line 9, and all other lines had been converted to it by 1942. Relays with proving contacts were used from 1928 onwards to provide added safety.

After 1945, it was necessary to renew the signalling and the opportunity was taken to adopt the internationally-accepted colours of red, yellow and green. Green distant signals were replaced by yellow aspects in March 1955 and in turn, green replaced white as the 'line clear' indication in April of the same year. More recently, the adoption of continuously-welded rail had made it necessary to adopt high-frequency current, at different frequencies in adjacent sections, for the signalling.

Today, the normal signal on the Métro is the two aspect colour light block (or 'spacing') signal, giving a green or red aspect according to the track circuit. At the entry to busier stations, three aspect signals are often found, in which a yellow indication allows entry to the station at reduced speed when the preceding train has just cleared it. In certain places, this signal is supplemented by a preceding intermediate signal, whose function is to anticipate the clearing of the station and which, when clear, allows a train to approach a station when the rear of the preceding train is half-way along the platform. These signals are generally protected by an outer two aspect signal, which remains at red when the other have cleared. On curves and other areas of reduced visibility, repeater signals are provided, giving yellow and green aspects only and are worked in conjunction with the block signal ahead. In all cases, a train is protected in the rear by two red signals, except at entry to stations as mentioned above.

Train stops have not been used at any time on the Métro, but since the days of the Hall signalling system, any train which has passed a signal at danger has set off a bell and a visual indication in the next station. These can be cut off only by the station staff and such incidents have to be reported in writing.

There were few shunting signals in the early days, but a system developed as terminal layouts grew more complex, quite independent of the running signals. Following a collision at Porte des Lilas in 1949, when a driver confused a shunting signal with a block signal and passed the latter at red, block signals have generally been removed from these areas, leaving only the shunting signals. These are generally rectangular, in contrast to the round block signals, and the two aspects are horizontal rather than vertical. There are also rectangular signals at points and crossovers, which show green for the main line and yellow for the branch, in each case with an arrow superimposed. A red indication is given

Left **A two-aspect automatic 'spacing' signal at Quai de la Rapée on line 5. Under the signal can be seen the 35kph speed restriction sign and immediately to the right the indication for service regulation and departure.**
R.J. Greenaway

Right **The south end of Créteil l'Echat station on line 8, looking in the direction of Créteil-Préfecture. Of interest are the semi-automatic (rectangular-shaped) signals (which have fibre optic lenses) and, immediately to the left of the letter A, a small white light indicating that the route reading over the points ahead is set and locked. On the far left, to the right of the 'Danger' notice can be seen 'ring-pull' equipment for discharging traction current.** *R.J. Greenaway*

only when the points are changing. There are also various fixed signals to indicate speed limits, etc., and markings by the trackside or on the tunnel walls (a white bar and circle on a dark background) warn of reduced visibility or restricted width.

At certain specially chosen locations in the open air, signal aspects are being renewed using fibre optic lenses. These, although very costly, give greatly improved sighting in conditions of poor visibility.

The maximum speed allowed on the Métro is 70kph, but this is only possible in the outer suburban sections, where stations are not so close together. Otherwise, the speed allowed is shown by illuminated signs, white on a dark background, and applies from speed restriction to speed restriction, or, if it applies first, the next station. Where the speed may be increased between stations, then this is also shown at the appropriate location.

At terminal stations, the signalling is worked by the local signal cabin, often situated on an overbridge with a view of the station. Here, according to the age of the location, a Chef de Manœuvre may have very modern push-button equipment for operating signals and points, or an old style lever frame, some of which are akin to 'beer handles'. Such examples of the latter still exist at Pont de Levallois (line 3), Châtelet (11), Porte de Montreuil and Mairie de Montreuil (9), Mairie d'Ivry (7) and Mairie d'Issy (12), but their days are numbered and will be replaced in the near future.

An illuminated diagram of the local area is provided, as well as a visual display unit, which shows the position of all trains bound for that terminus on the line, which greatly assists in the forward planning of departure regulation.

At intermediate reversing points along the line, there are two methods of operation. At selected sites, service reversing is performed automatically by the operation of a single switch in the control centre (PCC). The occupation of track circuits and the passage of trains is all that is needed for this system to operate. At other less important emergency reversing points, large levers by the trackside require manual intervention and operation, but authority to operate them is given by the control room. This system is also provided at the many interconnections between Métro lines.

Automatic Train Operation

The first experiments on the Métro with Automation Train Operation (ATO or Pilotage Automatique) were carried out from 1951 on the shuttle line (the 'Navette'), concurrently with the experiments with pneumatic tyres on, rolling stock. Passengers were carried on the single motor coach most weekday afternoons from 13 April 1952 to 31 May 1956, and the system proved to be totally safe and reliable in operation. However, the RATP recognised that there was a difference between testing this system on the quiet backwater of the Navette, and putting it into full operation on a line as busy as line 4. Unfortunately, there was not at that time the finance available to allow a more extensive trial and another decade was to elapse before the idea was revived.

In 1967, line 11 was equipped for ATO and two trains were equipped with the necessary apparatus. Again, there was complete success in operation and all trains were converted by 1969. From then, conversion of the other lines followed, the programme being concluded with line 2 in July 1979. Lines 10, 3bis and 7bis do not have service intervals that are sufficiently short to warrant the expense of conversion to automatic operation and have instead been converted to non-automatic one-person-operation.

The system of ATO used on the Métro is based on an induction cable, carrying current drawn from the signalling system and laid between the running rails to the 'Greek pattern'. The cable has a PVC covering and lies on a wooden surface, which is fixed to the sleepers. Messages transmitted by the cable are picked up by two collectors placed underneath the middle coach. The cable is divided into unequal segments, the length of which is defined by the speed of transmission of information and the speed of the train; the average length of time taken to traverse one section is 0.3 second. The cable carries two programmes, one for acceleration and one for braking. If a train passes through a section more quickly than it should do, the control equipment activates the brakes until the desired speed is reached; if it is going too slowly, it is made to accelerate. The control equipment itself takes up little space and is housed under one of the seats in the middle coach. In the early applications, it operated on the notches of the controller, but now the process is entirely electronic.

In conjunction with the introduction of programmed departures from terminal stations (q.v. below), the clock giving the departure time passes on information to the control equipment, which then requests the departure signal from the driver.

In service, ATO has proved to be very reliable. At stations, trains are brought to a halt within 500mm of the desired stopping point.

The ATO equipment on the Métro may be classified into two categories, which mainly differ by the frequency band of the electronic signals in between track and machine. Thus, there are the low frequency collecting systems in the 3 to 8kHz range, as used on the earliest lines (1, 3 and 4) and the 135kHz collecting systems on lines 2, 5, 6, 7, 8, 9, 11, 12 and 13. This latter system is the most recent and incorporates the latest technological advances, allowing a more flexible operating mode.

Lines were converted to ATO as follows:

September 1967	–	Line 11		June 1976	–	Line 8
February 1971	–	Line 4		April 1977	–	Line 13
February 1972	–	Line 1		July 1977	–	Line 7
July 1973	–	Line 3		December 1977	–	Line 12
February 1975	–	Line 6		April 1978	–	Line 5
May 1975	–	Line 9		July 1979	–	Line 2

When lines were being converted for ATO, the facility for full-speed manual driving was retained, and indeed, it is stipulated that the first train of the day must travel in normal manual mode. Where service intervals are less than two minutes, ATO is obligatory; service intervals in excess of four minutes demand manual driving. Between the two, the driver has a choice. Originally, ATO was obligatory, except for shunting, but following some shunting mishaps due to driver unfamiliarity, the system just described was introduced.

For those lines not equipped for ATO (10, 3bis and 7bis) and subsequently for manual driving on ATO lines, the system of controlled manual operation has been developed (CMC) especially for one-person-operated trains. This consists of a deadman's pedal and a ring around the controller handle, one of which must be operated every 30 seconds. If a driver omits to do so, a bell will sound in the cab, and if that does not have the desired effect in 2 ½ seconds, an emergency brake application follows. Cab signalling repeats the lineside signals, and again, if these are not observed, the brakes will be applied. This information is also transmitted to the control centre, which takes all the necessary steps in dealing with such situations.

All Métro rolling stock has, therefore, been equipped for CMC, as follows:

Line	Line Equipped	Stock Equipped	Completion
1	1983-84	1983-85	June 1985
2	1982-84	1981	February 1984
3	1981	1979-80	September 1981
4	1983-85	1982-84	June 1985
5	1983-84	1982-83	April 1985
6	1982-84	1982-83	April 1984
7	1982	1980-81	November 1982
8	1981	1980-81	May 1982
9	1983-84	1982-84	August 1984
10	1974-75	1975-76	1975-76
11	1981	1980-81	August 1981
12	1983	1983	November 1983
13	1980	1979-80	August 1980

Train Service Control

In former times, when the Métro operated with short trains and short interstation distances, the frequency of trains was comparatively low. However, as traffic has risen, it has been necessary to increase frequencies during busy times, and service regularity has become increasingly sensitive to even slight disturbances.

At the start it was incumbent on the supervising staff distributed over the lines to take appropriate corrective measures in the event of breakdowns. This often led to long, random and imprecise service intervals. Before the advent of the central control room, heavy rush hour traffic and subsequent extended station stops generated late running of services. On line 1, for example, the accumulated late running in the peaks under normal conditions was 22 minutes.

To enable more efficient control of trains, therefore, the RATP has, over a period of time, linked its Métro lines to a central control, or PCC (Poste de Commande Centralisée), where all operations are monitored. Rapid communications are provided in the form of telephone links to key locations, and a two-way high-frequency carrier wave radio between drivers and the PCC. An illuminated diagram for each line is provided, arranged in pairs, one above the other, where train movement can be observed by train numbers and track circuit occupation. In the event of a service disruption, the controllers have every facility to deal with the situation. This may vary from spacing out trains to allow equal but maximum loading, to reversing the service short of a breakdown and operating an emergency timetable. Each diagram has facilities to charge or discharge traction current, or to divide a section. Other facilities provided include signal telephone communications, control of the remaining portillon gates at platform entrances (the high service reliability of recent years, through central control, ATO, programmed departures and reduced station stop times, has made these almost unnecessary), and direct communication with station ticket offices. Although service regulation is carried out by computer, it is possible for manual intervention by the PCC. In either case, a train being held for regulation is indicated to the driver by three flashing white lights in a triangular shape, located adjacent to the station starting signal.

The PCC is located in Boulevard Bourdon, almost diagonally opposite the entrance to the closed station of Arsenal on line 5. It is within short walking distance of Bastille (lines 1, 5 and 8), Quai de la Rapée (5) and Sully Morland (7). The first line to be connected to PCC operation was line 1 on 15 June 1967, and immediately the peak accumulated late running on that line diminished from 22 minutes to just 2½ minutes. Other lines were subsequently linked to PCC operation, the last being achieved in 1975. Dates were as follows:

June 1967	–	Line 1
September 1967	–	Line 11
February 1969	–	Line 4
March 1969	–	Line 7
February 1970	–	Lines 3/3bis
October 1970	–	Line 9
May 1971	–	Line 8
September 1971	–	Line 12
May 1973	–	Line 2
June 1973	–	Line 5
July 1974	–	Line 13
July 1974	–	Line 14*
September 1974	–	Line 10
November 1974	–	Line 6
February 1975	–	Line 7bis

*Merged with line 13 on 9 November 1976.

The PCC actually comprises two large circular rooms, interconnected, one with lines 2, 5, 6, 10, 11 and 13, the other containing lines 1, 3/3bis, 4, 7/7bis, 8, 9 and 12.

The high standard of Métro service operating in recent years has rendered many of the portillon gates superfluous, but where they have been retained, they can normally be seen in the open position. Their operation was originally controlled by the passage of trains, but now they are controlled by the local station or the PCC. *John Thomason*

Programmed Departures

Until a few years ago, the minimum headways during peak hours were not less than 1min 50 sec. In order to reduce these minimum headways on which the carrying capacity of the Métro depends, the RATP came up with an operating principle known as 'Programmed Departures' from terminal stations. Under this system the operating instructions are displayed along successive stations, on a digital clock face telling drivers of each train the 'staggered terminal departure time'. This is the actual time (expressed only in minutes and seconds), less the theoretical travel time between the departure terminal and the considered station. Thus, to follow the timetable, the driver has to leave the station when the time displayed coincides with the terminal departure time. For example, with a train that leaves the terminal at, say 08.05.15, the driver should depart from the stations along the route when the clock displays 05 15. Each clock also gives the type of running schedule then in operation, which differs during the course of the day. There are four different running times – Heaviest flow peak (marche 'A'), counterflow peak ('B'), midday off-peak ('C') and evening off-peak ('D').

Drivers are kept advised of the permissible dwell time in stations by means of a buzzer, triggered by computer or manually from the PCC. The driver then activates the door closing button which, in turn, activates a pleasant audible sound over the doors, warning passengers of the imminent closing of the doors by a second push on the same button. When a train arrives at a station with a delay exceeding a given threshold, the sound warning by buzzer is given a few seconds in advance of the permissible dwell time to enable the train to absorb its delay a little at a time.

The programmed departures system, first put into use on line 7 in 1969, is now operative on all lines except 10, 11, 3bis and 7bis. By this means, it has been possible to increase the number of trains by shortening the headways (to as little as 1min 35sec), thus raising the line capacity by 15–20%, without changing the signalling system.

Timetables

Train services on the Métro are timetabled to a precision of five seconds. There are three different services provided within the seven-day week: Mondays to Fridays, Saturdays and Sundays.

On Mondays to Fridays, there are four schedules operated throughout the year. The full service timetable operates from October to April. During May, June and September, a slightly reduced service is provided on most lines, followed by a further reduction for the month of July. The fourth and lowest level of service applies during the month of August, when many Parisians leave the capital for their annual holiday. It should be noted at this stage that, generally, fewer trains operate in the morning peak due to the protracted nature of the morning rush period. In the evening peak, however, where the busy period is more concentrated, the maximum service is operated. For example, the four different service levels for line 5 are as follows; the figures show the number of trains in service for each period and the scheduled service interval:

	Morning Peak		Midday		Evening Peak		Evening Off-peak	
Full Service	39	1 min 55 sec	24	3 min 20 sec	45	1 min 45 sec	10	8 min 15 sec
First Reduction	35	2 min 10 sec	22	3 min 40 sec	40	1 min 55 sec	10	8 min 15 sec
July	29	2 min 40 sec	19	4 min 20 sec	32	2 min 30 sec	10	8 min 15 sec
August	22	3 min 40 sec	15	5 min 0 sec	27	3 min 0 sec	10	8 min 15 sec

It will thus be appreciated that the evening service provided is unchanged throughout the year. This applies, too, on Saturday and Sunday services, of which there are two of each type, being winter (generally October to May) and summer (June to September). On both Saturdays and Sundays, an afternoon 'busy' service is provided, usually from about 14.30 to 18.00. On Sunday mornings before about 09.00, a service similar to the evenings is operated.

	08.00 to 09.00		Morning		Afternoon Busy		Evening Off-peak	
Winter Service	16	5 min 5 sec	17	4 min 45 sec	22	3 min 45 sec	10	8 min 15 sec
Summer Service	14	6 min 0 sec	14	6 min 0 sec	16	5 min 20 sec	10	8 min 15 sec

	05.30 to 06.30		Morning		Afternoon Busy		Evening Off-peak	
Winter Service	11	8 min 0 sec	15	5 min 35 sec	17	4 min 45 sec	10	8 min 15 sec
Summer Service	11	8 min 0 sec	12	7 min 15 sec	14	5 min 45 sec	10	8 min 15 sec

The Paris Métro operates from 05.30 daily, when the first trains depart from the terminal stations. At some former terminal stations, for example, on line 9 at 05.30, trains start from the two termini (Pont de Sèvres and Mairie de Montreuil) as well as from République (both directions), Porte de Saint-Cloud (going east) and Porte de Montreuil (going west). At night, the last trains arrive at the terminal stations at 01.15. Because of the short distances between stations, the complex network of lines, and complex interchange corridors, there are no last train connections between the various Métro lines. In common with other European systems, the Paris Métro is a 365-day-a-year underground railway network – even a good service is provided on Christmas Day with the operation of Sunday schedules from the usual 05.30 to 01.15. The UK public transport operators seem to be something of an exception at Christmas time!

To give an appreciation of the level of Métro services, the trains in service and scheduled frequencies on the Monday to Friday full winter service are given in the following table:

Summary of Monday to Friday Winter Services

Line	No. of Daily Deps	Section		Morning Peak		Midday Off-peak		Evening Peak		Evening Off-peak
1	355	Château de Vincennes to Pont de Neuilly	37	2 min 00 sec	23	3 min 25 sec	42	1 min 45 sec	10	7 min 55 sec
2	343	Nation to Porte Dauphine	35	2 min 00 sec	22	3 min 20 sec	40	1 min 50 sec	9	8 min 15 sec
3	338	Pont de Levallois to Galliéni	32	2 min 10 sec	21	3 min 30 sec	39	1 min 45 sec	9	8 min 30 sec
3b	259	Porte des Lilas to Gambetta	4	3 min 15 sec	3	4 min 15 sec	4	3 min 00 sec	2	8 min 30 sec
4	423	Porte de Clignancourt to Porte d'Orléans	40	1 min 40 sec	23	3 min 00 sec	44	1 min 35 sec	10	7 min 00 sec
5	350	Place d'Italie to Bobigny	39	1 min 55 sec	24	3 min 20 sec	45	1 min 45 sec	10	8 min 15 sec
6	335	Charles de Gaulle-Étoile to Nation	34	2 min 05 sec	20	3 min 45 sec	38	1 min 50 sec	10	7 min 30 sec
7	384	La Courneuve to Maison Blanche	60 {	1 min 45 sec	32 {	3 min 30 sec	65 {	1 min 40 sec	19 {	6 min 00 sec
		Maison Blanche to Ivry/ Villejuif		3 min 30 sec		7 min 00 sec		3 min 20 sec		12 min 00 sec
7b	215	Louis Blanc to Pré-Saint-Gervais	6	4 min 10 sec	5	4 min 30 sec	6	4 min 10 sec	3	8 min 45 sec
8	312	Balard to M.A.-les Juilliottes	46 {	2 min 15 sec	30 {	3 min 40 sec	51 {	2 min 10 sec	14 {	8 min 30 sec
		M.A.-les Juilliottes to Créteil		4 min 30 sec		7 min 20 sec		*		8 min 30 sec
9	358	Pont de Sèvres to Mairie de Montreuil	53	1 min 55 sec	32	3 min 35 sec	61	1 min 45 sec	16	7 min 30 sec
10	271	Austerlitz to Porte d'Auteuil	20 {	3 min 10 sec	17 {	3 min 45 sec	23 {	2 min 45 sec	8 {	8 min 45 sec
		Porte d'Auteil to Boulogne		6 min 20 sec		7 min 30 sec		5 min 30 sec		8 min 45 sec
11	309	Châtelet to Mairie des Lilas	16	2 min 20 sec	9	4 min 15 sec	18	2 min 05 sec	6	6 min 45 sec
12	305	Porte de la Chapelle to Mairie d'Issy	32	2 min 35 sec	24	3 min 30 sec	34	2 min 20 sec	12	7 min 00 sec
13	396	Châtillon-Montrouge to La Fourche	46 {	1 min 50 sec	23 {	3 min 45 sec	48 {	1 min 45 sec	14 {	6 min 00 sec
		La Fourche to Gabriel Péri		5 min 30 sec		7 min 30 sec		5 min 15 sec		12 min 00 sec
		La Fourche to Saint-Denis		†		7 min 30 sec		†		12 min 00 sec

* Interval is 4 min 20 sec before 17.30, 2 min 10 sec thereafter.

† Two trains every 5 min 30 sec (morning peak), 5 min 15 sec (evening peak).

Track

The rails used on the Métro have always been highly standardised. Vignoles rail of a weight of 52kg/m was used on line 1 when it was built. These rails were 15 metres long, but when line 2 was constructed, rails 18 metres long were used and this length has remained standard ever since. The rails are laid on sleepers at the rate of one sleeper every 750mm. They are fastened down with sleeper screws and are joined together with fishplates. The track is embedded in a ballast of crushed stone. On recent extensions, a concrete trackbed with rubber inserts has been used. This latter type of construction is thought to absorb vibration more readily than the traditional permanent way and, as less attention need be paid to levelling, it is easier and quicker to instal.

The Nord-Sud has a more individual elastic approach, probably adopted because of the sharp curvature of line 12. It used bullhead rails, slightly deeper than those of the CMP (165mm as against 150mm) which were supported by chairs incorporating a cushion of linoleum and fixed to the sleepers with a cork insert. The sleepers on the Nord-Sud were spaced at a greater distance apart than on the CMP – 1.40m as against 750mm. Unfortunately the linoleum and cork inserts soon lost their elasticity and disintegrated, causing vertical movements in the track and severe corrugation. Such track had a short life and was quickly replaced by standard construction after the merger with the CMP in 1930.

Welding of running rails was not adopted until 1960, since traditional methods allowed for speedy replacement. However, welding was adopted when line 1 was converted to 'pneu' operation and its advantages were such that it was soon adopted for all lines and by 1980 most track was of welded construction. Only at curves and crossings and on the elevated sections of lines 2 and 6 are traditional methods still used, in the latter case to avoid placing undue stress on the pillars of the viaducts. Rails on curves generally have to be replaced every three years, but elsewhere they normally have a life of 15-20 years.

Because of the normal end-to-end method of operation of most Métro lines, the number of points and crossovers, apart from terminal areas, is relatively limited. Only lines 7, 10 and 13 have junctions (at Maison Blanche, Auteuil and La Fourche respectively), but all of these are arranged to avoid the crossing of lines on the flat, a 'flying junction' arrangement being constructed to avoid the confliction of lines. Many points are normally fixed in the straight position, and often facing points instead of trailing points are used. Points at terminal stations have been electrically controlled since 1911, and many crossovers on the line of route have been similarly equipped since the PCC system of control was introduced from 1967. There remain, however, a number of hand-worked points at locations considered as less important, and at the interline connections. Authority for the use of these points is given by the PCC.

The third rail was originally bullhead of 38kg/m but this was very quickly changed to a much heavier Vignoles rail, then again to the present 'T' section rail of 52kg/m. It is placed at a distance of 330mm from the running rail and is fixed by means of porcelain or basalt insulators to every fourth sleeper. Traction current returns via the running rails, which have to be bonded.

It should be noted that the actual track gauge of the Métro is fractionally wider than standard, at 1.44m. In contrast, the spacing between the tracks is only 1.33m, as opposed to main line railways standard of 1.85m.

The track used by rubber-tyred 'pneu' trains consists of two broad 'I' beams of metal, each 300mm wide, placed outside the normal running rails, at a distance from centre to centre of 1.98m. On line 11, much of the original 'pneu' trackwork was originally of tropical hardwood, but this was replaced during track renewal in 1982–83. Reinforced concrete surfaces are sometimes used in stations and, on the elevated sections of line 6, they are ribbed to improve adhesion in wet or frosty weather. Outside the 'I' beams, two lateral bars support the horizontal guide wheels, which also serve as the positive current rails. The ordinary running rails are retained, as are points and crossings, where the beams are interrupted. If a tyre should lose pressure in service (which is a very unusual occurrence) then the train will automatically switch to the use of these rails. The conventional running rails also act for current return and shoes from the train make continuous contact with them, hence them remaining in shiny condition. Conventional rolling stock can therefore operate on 'pneu' lines, but a special lateral current collector shoe has to be fitted.

Electricity Supply and Distribution

It used to be that most of the electric power supplied for Métro operation was provided in the form of high voltage alternating current from three plants and two Électricité de France (EDF) substations located at Saint-Denis, Ivry, Billancourt, Vitry Nord and Arceuil. Three-phase 10,000 volt cables led from the EDF plants to various substations, where the power was stepped down and converted into 600V dc for the Métro, and to 1,500V dc for the Ligne de Sceaux (now RER line B). High voltage cubicles, many of which were located in the substations, make up the grid of the power system.

In 1979 the total revamping of the urban electrical power supply system was completed. High voltage supplied by the EDF from the 63kV grid in the Greater Paris region, to four stations at Monttessuy, Père Lachaise A and B, Lamarck and Denfert, was distributed throughout Paris and from the 225kV grid to three further stations at Père Lachaise C, René Coty and Ney. All these high-voltage stations step down to 15,000 volts for distribution to 138 rectifier substations equipped with medium voltage silicon rectifiers (1,750 to 4,500kW). In addition, given the distance from the high voltage RATP stations, 19 rectifier substations are directly fed from the EDF at 20kV.

The rectifier substations feed the 750 volt and 1,500 volt traction current supplies, so spaced that any one of them can be shut down without detriment, the other surrounding rectifier substations supplying the required replacement power due to their diversity. In each rectifier substation the equipment making up the substation is separated into readily removable, interchangeable and transportable units. Each unit is of standard modules so that in event of a breakdown, it is possible to replace the defective equipment without delay, by means of specially equipped breakdown vehicles.

Power is also distributed to 523 stepdown transformer units (15kV/380–220 volts) feeding power to the electrical installations in tunnels and at stations, as well as to sundry administrative buildings, bus garages and workshops.

The station lighting circuits are fed from transformer substations located in 'power and lighting stations'. For reasons of security there are two entirely separate sources of supply. In the event of failure of the overall RATP power system, standby electric generating sets are remote controlled from the Electrical Control Room (PCE – which actually adjoins the Métro PCC), which clusters together all of the high voltage station controls. In addition, batteries are installed locally in stations to provide spaced-out lighting along the tracks in case of mains power failure.

Substations on the Métro are generally about 3km apart. For ease of identification in the PCC, current sections are named and numbered. If current is required for any reason, then the tracks in both directions have to be isolated. On the main running lines, it is not possible to isolate just one track, although there is the facility to divide a section to enable an emergency crossover to be used, should it be in the current section with the problem, but away from the actual problem itself. On the other hand, extensive isolation facilities exist at terminal stations, where there are often a number of stabling sidings. Facilities exist on every Métro platform for passengers to discharge traction current. These are contained in a cabinet which has other passenger aids (such as communication with the station supervisor, and a fire extinguisher) and are protected by a glass screen; a pull-ring automatically cuts off the current. These pull-rings are also located in tunnels, spaced at 50 metre intervals.

At night, current is only taken off on the Métro when work in the tunnels or on the track is scheduled. The system must therefore be regarded as 'live' all the time.

Tunnels

Generally in Paris, Métro tunnels have been made as shallow as possible. Only on lines constructed later did these go to any great depth, and this was for the reason of passing under existing lines when they were crossed. New extensions into the suburbs are also built just below the surface.

Some of the Métro was originally built by the 'cut and cover' method, such stations being recognised by their girder roofs. Almost all of the tunnel extensions from the 1970s have been built by this method, where a trench is dug out, the route constructed, and then covered over again. However, much of the original Métro was constructed by the 'Belgian Method'. In this method, a pilot gallery is cut following the line of the upper part of the main tunnel. Shafts are dug to this at intervals for the removal of the spoil. From this gallery, by digging sideways and supporting the earth above by props and wooden planks, space is obtained for building the roof of the tunnel with masonry. Under this roof the gallery can be widened into a covered trench along the line of the tunnel. From this trench, every few metres, side trenches are dug to where the walls are to be built. The walls, also of masonry, are built under the roof, giving a masonry arch tunnel, of 'basket handle' cross section, resting on concrete footings. The whole of the tunnel cross-section is then excavated. The tunnel floor, or invert, of concrete, is next added. The invert is slightly curved in dry ground, or more curved if water is present, in which case it is also waterproofed. Finally, liquid cement is injected behind the masonry work of the tunnel, to fill any voids left by the compression of the soil.

A number of crossings of the River Seine are made in tunnel. These include:

Line 4 between Châtelet and Cité, and between Cité and Saint Michel, both in a double track tunnel formed of a sunken caisson in a trench in the river bed.

Line 10 between Javel and Mirabeau, constructed as previously described.

Line 7 between Sully-Morland and Jussieu is in a double-track shield-driven tube, of cast iron segments, 7.25m internal diameter, as is line 8 between Concorde and Invalides.

Line 12, between Concorde and Chambre des Députés, is in two single track shield-driven tubes of 5m diameter.

The most recently built crossing under the Seine is on line 13 between Invalides and Champs-Élysées-Clémenceau, opened in 1976.

Depots and Stabling Points

A feature of Paris Métro rolling stock depots is that they are used only for train maintenance and not for stabling trains during slack periods or at weekends. Trains not required for maintenance are stabled 'on the line' at numerous positions, generally at terminal stations on each line. Each line of the Métro has a depot for routine mainte- nance, and some of these have been specially adapted for repairs and major overhauls. The depots and their locations are as follows:

Line 1   FONTENAY (east of terminus Château de Vincennes)
Line 2   CHARONNE (east of Nation)
Line 3   SAINT FARGEAU (east of Gambetta)
Line 4   SAINT OUEN (north of Porte de Clignancourt)
Line 5   BOBIGNY (between the two Bobigny stations – opened April 1988)
Line 6   PLACE D'ITALIE
Line 7   CHOISY (access from Porte de Choisy)
Line 8   JAVEL (access from Lourmel)
Line 9   BOULOGNE (access from Pont de Sèvres)
Line 10 PORTE D'AUTEUIL
Line 11 MAIRIE DES LILAS (east of station)
Line 12 VAUGIRARD (access from Porte de Versailles)
Line 13 PLEYEL (access from Carrefour Pleyel)

In addition, the depot for engineers' trains is located at VILLETTE, near to Porte de la Villette at the northern part of line 7, with maintenance of engineers' vehicles being undertaken also at Vaugirard depot.

Three of the above depots are in fact located underground, these being Porte d'Auteuil, Mairie des Lilas and Pleyel. All of the maintenance depots have inspection pits. Most also have lifting facilities and some have travelling cranes to move equipment around the depot area. Three of the depots have been adapted to perform major overhauls. These are at Fontenay (which deals with all 'pneu' stock), Choisy (the first generation of modern steel-wheel-on-steel-rail trains – the MF67), and Saint Ouen (the latest of modern stock – the MF77, and, until recently, the old articulated stock, the MA52). During heavy overhaul, the cars are lifted to allow disassembly and inspection of the major components, such as axles, traction motors, bogies and compressors. There are specialised areas dealing with axle and bogie frame refurbishing, sheet metal work and welding, battery servicing and seat covering repairs. Motor cars undergo a major overhaul at 400,000km intervals, while trailers are overhauled every 500,000km. Painting of the car bodies is not always done to correspond with overhauls. Indeed, intervals between repaints varies from about every 11 years on trains which have some outside running, to about every 17 years on trains which run continuously in tunnel.

A view of Choisy depot on line 7, which deals with routine maintenance of that line's MF 77 stock, visible in the background. Note the three-way point in the foreground. Choisy depot also performs major overhauls on MF67 stock.
Brian Hardy

The underground depot at Porte d'Auteuil on line 10 deals only with routine maintenance of the articulated MA52 stock, and the handful of MF67 trains allocated to that line. MA52 unit E030, with motor car D59 nearest the camera, shows the Scharfenberg automatic coupler.
R.J. Greenaway

Above Vaugirard depot on line 12 was originally a Nord-Sud depot, and now deals with routine maintenance on line 12's MF67 stock, an example of which is seen in the centre. It also services the miscellaneous vehicle fleet used on works trains. The depot has rail access to the SNCF main line system and is used for new stock deliveries and the removal of old stock for scrap. For shunting these trains an ex-Nord-Sud pilot motor (TA03) can be seen on the left.   *Brian Hardy*

The stabling sidings at Bobigny on line 5, provide the stock for over two-thirds of the service, all being above ground without protection from the weather. During adverse winter weather, trains for service are sometimes stabled in the tunnels at Église de Pantin (the former terminus) and Porte de Pantin.
R.J. Greenaway

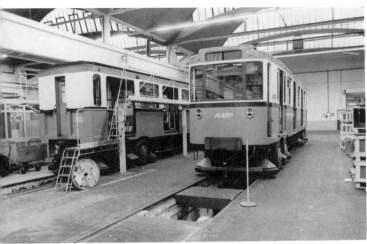

The depot at Fontenay on line 1, located beyond the terminus of Château de Vincennes, not only deals with routine maintenance of line 1's MP59 stock, but major overhauls of all 'pneu' stock. An MP55 driving motor car (right) from line 11 and an MP73 motor car (left) from line 6 undergo attention in February 1988.
R.J. Greenaway

Although the MF67 stock is overhauled at Choisy, repaints are undertaken at Fontenay where a type 'E' car is seen.
R.J. Greenaway

An interior view of an MF67 car at Fontenay depot, prior to re-painting, showing the seats removed. Two floor-to-ceiling grab poles are situated at each doorway position.
R.J. Greenaway

Returning now to trains stabled 'on the line', each terminal area has a number of specified locations where it is possible to stable trains. Crews are informed of the train's location by referring to a green chalkboard, which is updated by the terminal station supervisor. Trains are generally identified on these boards by the centre (first class) car, and in the train formations (pages 94-100) they are usually arranged in numerical order of these cars. Identification of the stabling location is by numbers and letters and in places which have more than one arrival and departure platform, these are often used to stable trains, during the day. Often, a serviceable spare train is kept ready to changeover any train that may become defective.

Only trains requiring maintenance actually go to depots on the Métro; trains not otherwise required are stabled on the line, and at each location a green chalkboard gives the stabling locations, updated as necessary. That for Mairie des Lilas and Porte des Lilas is seen on 18 February 1988, each rectangle representing a train's berth.
R.J. Greenaway

Stabling locations are identified by numbers and letters, and when occupying spare platforms the location may be found on the station wall. At Porte des Lilas on line 11 an MP55 train is stabled at position 1–1B (left) while the cab of an MP73 train is stabled at position Q–1B (right). *R.J. Greenaway*

The following table lists the maximum number of trains required for service on each line:

Line 1			**Line 7bis**	
Pont de Neuilly	3		Pré-Saint-Gervais	6
Porte Maillot	10			6
Château de Vincennes	29			
	42		**Line 8**	
			Balard	9
Line 2			Lourmel	4
Porte Dauphine	6		République	4
Nation	34		Maisons-Alfort-les	
	40		Juilliottes	15
			Créteil-Préfecture	19
Line 3				51
Galliéni	10			
Porte des Lilas (3bis)	13		**Line 9**	
Porte de Champerret	12		Pont de Sèvres	10
Pont de Levallois	4		Porte de Saint-Cloud	26
	39		République	2
			Porte de Montreuil	7
Line 3bis			Mairie de Montreuil	16
Porte des Lilas	4			61
	4			
			Line 10	
Line 4			Gare d'Austerlitz	8
Porte de Clignancourt	28		Porte d'Auteuil	15
Porte d'Orléans	16			23
	44			
			Line 11	
Line 5			Châtelet	8
Bobigny	31		Porte des Lilas	6
Église de Pantin	5		Mairie des Lilas	4
Place d'Italie	9			18
	45			
			Line 12	
Line 6			Porte de la Chapelle	12
Nation	15		Porte de Versailles	10
Place d'Italie	8		Mairie d'Issy	12
Kléber	15			34
	38			
			Line 13	
Line 7			Gabriel Péri	7
La Courneuve	13		Porte de Clichy	3
Porte de la Villette	20		Saint-Denis-Basilique	3
Porte d'Ivry	9		Carrefour Pleyel	7
Mairie d'Ivry	10		Invalides	11
Villejuif-Louis Aragon	13		Châtillon-Montrouge	17
	65			48

In addition, it is possible to stable trains at certain sidings located around the Métro system, as follows: *Line 1* Port Maillot; *Line 2* Blanche, Belleville; *Line 3* Arts et Métiers; *Line 4* Etienne Marcel, Saint Germain des Prés; *Line 6* Bercy, Edgar Quinet; *Line 7* Cadet, Pont Neuf; *Line 8* Concorde (bay platform); *Line 9* Alma Marceau; *Line 12* Trinité, Montparnasse-Bienvenüe.

Former terminal stations continue to have stabling areas for trains, as follows: *Line 5* Porte de Pantin; *Line 8* Charenton Ecoles, Porte de Charenton; *Line 13* Porte de Saint-Ouen, Porte de Vanves.

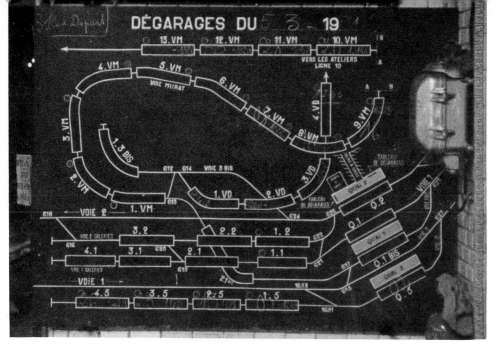

One of the more complex of stabling areas is at Porte de Saint-Cloud on line 9, photographed in 1981 before the reduction of tracks through the station area from five to four. A total of 34 stabling positions were available then, mainly in nearby tunnels.

R.J. Greenaway

Terminal Stations
Even from the very beginnings of the Métro, the facilities provided at terminal stations were variable. Now, with 13 main lines and two branches there is even greater variety, which provides much operational interest to the student of underground railways:

1. Reversing Beyond Station
Here, there are separate arrival and departure platforms and trains reversing have to proceed to a shunting neck, at which there is a narrow platform walkway (called a 'Trottoir') for drivers to change ends. In quiet periods, it is possible for the train operator to change ends and take the same train on its next journey. During peak periods, a number of shunting operators may be available to speed up operations – necessary when service intervals as frequent as 1min 40sec are being worked.

There are several variations to this method of working at terminal stations. The arrival platform may be served by two tracks, in which case trains may be accepted at intervals which are nearly as short as the time required to empty a train in peak hours. On the other hand, if the departure platform has two tracks (and there are instances where terminal stations have two tracks on arrival and departure), then the interval between departing trains may be shortened, or a spare train may be kept at one platform, ready to leave to fill a gap in the service caused by late running, or to replace a failed train. One track at the terminal station usually has an inspection pit, to allow maintenance staff to examine trains.

The above arrangements apply to: Château de Vincennes and Pont de Neuilly (line 1), Galliéni* and Pont de Levallois (line 3), Bobigny-Pablo Picasso* and Place d'Italie (line 5), La Courneuve †, Mairie d'Ivry and Villejuif - Louis Aragon* (line 7), Balard and Créteil-Préfecture† (line 8), Pont de Sèvres* and Mairie de Montreuil (line 9), Gare d'Austerlitz (line 10), Châtelet and Mairie des Lilas* (line 11), Porte de la Chapelle† and Mairie d'Issy (line 12), Châtillon-Montrouge †, Saint-Denis-Basilique* and Gabriel Péri (line 13).

At locations marked (*), it is possible for trains to run direct into the departure platform, or into a middle platform (†), to speed up turn round time during service difficulties, or during certain off-peak periods of operation.

One other station with shunting arrangements, but of an unusual nature, is at Louis Blanc on line 7bis, which offers cross-platform interchange with services on line 7. In fact the station comprises two separate sections – southbound on top of northbound. Trains from Pré-Saint-Gervais enter the southbound platform and a shunt operator takes the train out again, once passengers have alighted, clear of the points which then lead to the northbound, into which platform the incoming operator brings the train.

2. Non-Passenger Loops

In this arrangement, trains detrain in the arrival platform and then proceed empty via a loop to the departure platform. This eliminates the need for drivers to change ends and allows scheduled departures at as little as 1min 35sec intervals to be operated, especially on line 4, the busiest on the Métro. It also allows a number of trains to be in the loop at the same time and this facilitates the regulation of the service, as the interval between planned and possible departure times can be observed and adjusted as necessary.

Locations with this arrangement are Porte Dauphine* (line 2), Porte des Lilas‡ (line 3bis), Porte de Clignancourt and Porte d'Orléans‡* (line 4).

At locations marked (*) it is possible to run direct into the departure platform, while at terminal stations marked (‡) there is also a 'Trottoir' provided, which can be used as an alternative to the loop.

3. Passenger Loops

These are perhaps the most interesting of the terminal station arrangements, as far as the enthusiast is concerned, with the warren of tunnels and sidings, and trains weaving in between stabled trains. These exist at Nation (line 2), Charles de Gaulle-Étoile and Nation (line 6), Pré-Saint-Gervais (line 7bis) and Porte d'Auteuil (line 10). Unlike the two previous operations described above, the passenger loops often aggrevate any irregularities in the service.

Interesting operating alternatives are available at the two loops on line 6. At Charles de Gaulle-Étoile, with only one track at the station, separate arrival and departure platforms are provided. However, due to the restricted nature of this arrangement, trains do not take their layover time here – this is done at the next station in the southbound direction, at Kléber, which has two island platforms, one for each direction. It is also possible for a train to reverse at Étoile and travel back on the northbound line, gaining its correct track at Kléber.

The loop at Nation on line 6 is in fact only used in the peaks by departing trains. At other times, when trains are stabled on this loop, reversing service trains can either proceed forward to the 'Trottoir', or reverse at one side of the terminal island platforms.

4. Dead-End Terminal Stations

There are only two terminal stations on the Métro which do not have tracks going beyond the platforms, in either sidings or loops. These are at Gambetta (line 3bis) and Boulogne – Pont de Saint-Cloud (line 10), both being island platforms with a track each side. At the former location, this platform was originally used by trains on line 3 proceeding to Paris, cut short when branch line 3bis was created in 1971 so that the main line 3 could serve the then newly built extension to Galliéni. The present connecting subway between the line 3bis platforms and the new Gambetta station on line 3 (Paris direction) uses the tunnel formerly occupied by the Métro.

Interline Connections

The number of non-passenger connections between Métro lines is numerous and no one Métro line is totally isolated, even though a number of connections may have to be used to reach the ultimate destination. The most frequent use of the connections is made by works trains at night, most of which start their journey in the small hours from the depot near Porte de la Villette on line 7, after the last train has arrived at 01.15. The connections are also used, but to a lesser extent, by stock transfers between lines and for overhauls and maintenance.

The length of the connections, of course, varies with the location, but can be as long as 1.83km between lines 9 and 10 from Porte de Saint-Cloud to Auteuil via the never opened station of Porte Molitor, or as short as the length of a pair of points, such as between lines 5 and 7 side by side at Gare de l'Est. The various line connections are as follows:

Connecting Lines	At/Between
1—6	Charles de Gaulle-Étoile
1—8	Champs-Élysées Clémenceau (1) and Concorde (8)
1—5	Gare de Lyon (1) and Quai de la Rapée (5)
1—2	Nation
1—6	Nation
2—4—5	Anvers (2) and Gare du Nord (4 and 5)
2—3	Père-Lachaise
2—9	Nation
3—7	Opéra
3—11	Réaumur Sebastopol (3) and Arts et Métiers (11)
3—5	République
3—3b	Gambetta
3b—7b*	Porte des Lilas (3b) and Place des Fêtes (7b)
3b—7b	Porte des Lilas (3b) and Pré-Saint-Gervais (7b)
4—10	Odéon (4) and Cluny La Sorbonne (10)
4—12	Vavin (4) and Montparnasse-Bienvenüe (12)
4—6	Vavin (4) and Edgar Quinet (6)
5—7	Gare de l'Est
5—8	République
6—9†	Trocadéro
6—8*	Daumesnil
5—6—7	Place d'Italie
7—10	Place Monge (7) and Maubert-Mutualité (10)
7—7b†	Louis Blanc
8—9	République
8—10	La Motte-Picquet
8—13	Invalides
9—10*	Porte de Saint-Cloud (9) and Auteuil (10)
9—10	Michel-Ange-Auteuil
12—13	Montparnasse-Bienvenüe
12—13	Saint-Lazare

Notes: * Used for stabling trains
       † Two separate connections, one in each direction

A view looking west from the reopened station of Cluny la Sorbonne on line 10 in February 1988 showing (left) the eastbound line to Gare d'Austerlitz and (right) the westbound line to Porte d'Auteuil/Boulogne. The centre track is one of the numerous interline connections on the Métro which in this case connects with line 4 to Odeon.
R.J. Greenaway

CHAPTER 4
STATIONS

The growth of the Métro has already been described in Chapter II, and at the beginning of September 1939 the system comprised 159km. The start of the Second World War saw the system reduced in operational size to just over 92km, with only 85 stations open to the public. Some lines were closed completely, while many stations and sections of line were closed.

Indeed, some stations encountered two or three periods of closure, but Saint Sulpice on line 4 was closed on no less than four separate occasions. At the end of 1945 there were still 73 Métro stations closed, of which 43 reopened in 1946 and 13 more in 1947. A further seven were eventually reopened in 1951, but this left a further ten still outstanding:

Arsenal (line 5)	Cluny (10)	Rennes (12)
Bel-Air (6)	Croix Rouge (10)	Saint Martin (8 & 9)
Champ de Mars (8)	Liège (13)	Varenne (14)

Over a decade followed before two further stations were reopened: Varenne (on 24 December 1962) and Bel-Air (on 7 January 1963). However, it was on 29 June 1967 that the fate of the eight remaining stations was decided by the RATP. Two were to reopen (Liège on 20 May 1968 and Rennes on 16 September 1968, but both on Mondays to Saturdays only and until 20.00), but it was intended that the other six were to remain closed permanently. One subsequent exception to this was the station of Cluny, which later featured in plans to be linked to the Saint-Michel station complex on RER lines B and C. It reopened on 17 February 1988, named Cluny la Sorbonne.

Cluny station on line 10, which closed in September 1939, was reopened on 17 February 1988 as Cluny la Sorbonne, giving interchange with RER lines B and C. On the ceiling are mosaic patterns of birds and signatures of famous names connected with Sorbonne University. The three-track arrangement here is somewhat unusual, the centre one being used for stock transfers between lines 10 and 4. *R.J. Greenaway*

Design and Presentation

The original stations of the CMP possessed a unity of style, which apart from reducing construction costs, would have delighted any design consultant, had there been such around in the early 1900s. The walls were lined with white tiles, relieved only by the station names which were white on a blue ground, in either tiled form or on plates, by the maroon bench seats and by advertisements, though in the general gloom these would not have been much noticed. Lighting was by clusters of incandescent lamps which were described as 'brilliant'. Having established these standards, the CMP then stuck to them for the first four decades of its existence. Although there was great consistency, stations that were built to the cut and cover method were instantly recognisable by the girders at roof level, whereas other stations had white tiles extended right over the station ceiling. It was not until 1937, by which time ideas of brilliance had obviously changed, that the first attempts were made to improve the lighting, mainly in those stations dealing with traffic to the international exhibition of that year. But neither this nor the post-war experiments with fluorescent lighting did anything for the general image of the Métro as conveyed to the public in its stations. It also did not help that the ticket collectors' booths and the ticket offices were painted black.

An original type of Métro station on line 9 with tiled names and advertisement surrounds.   *R.J. Greenaway*

Some station names are on curved enamel plates rather than in tile form, but these are now in the minority. Note the bevelled white tiles which are a tradition on Paris Métro stations.
R.J. Greenaway

The Nord-Sud company had done rather better in its presentation of stations. The roofs were decorated with patterns of occasional green or brown tiles and the advertisement panels were similarly framed, with the company's N–S entwined logo incorporated in the design. Over the station tunnel mouths, similar tiles picked out the name of the terminal station then in use. This accounts for some stations on line 12 having 'Direction Montmartre' or 'Direction Montparnasse' instead of Porte de Versailles or Porte de la Chapelle, the line having opened in stages. Another interesting feature of the Nord-Sud was the rotunda forming the ticket hall of Saint-Lazare, which was of considerable merit. It is gratifying that the RATP has restored two of these stations to their former glory, Liège on line 13 and Pasteur on line 12.

Above **The stations of the Nord-Sud company were more decoratively finished than those of the CMP. Pasteur on line 12 in January 1961 shows the bands of brown tiles which continue over the roof of the station.** *RATP*

The tiled surrounds to station names and advert borders on Nord-Sud stations include the company's entwined 'NS' initials. *R.J. Greenaway*

Another Nord-Sud feature was the name of the terminal station over the headwall, this example being on line 13. Although still in situ at some stations, Porte de Saint-Ouen ceased to be a terminus in 1952. *R.J. Greenaway*

In the early post-war years, it was recognised that the general appearance of stations was no longer in keeping with contemporary standards of design, but at first no money was available for general improvement, other than the installation of fluorescent lighting. After some unsuccessful experiments, this was developed to a reliable standard and was generally adopted in the 1950s.

The first complete rebuilding of stations was done on a very individualistic basis, the aim being to give each station its own atmosphere and to break totally with the unity of the past. Six stations were thus modernised between 1952 and 1958. The first to be so treated was Franklin D. Roosevelt on line 9, which in 1952 was completely refurbished using unpainted aluminium panelling and illuminated advertisements. This was followed in 1954 with stainless steel cladding for Opéra on line 3, while in 1955 Chaussée d'Antin (line 9) was modernised in a further different style, followed by Saint-Paul (line 1) in 1956. In 1957 the line 1 platforms at Franklin D. Roosevelt were refurbished in glass and aluminium, the remaining painted sections being rendered in orange-red and blue. Over thirty years later, in 1987, the result here is still bold and attractive. To mark the completion of this station, a banquet was held on the platforms of line 1 after the trains had stopped for the night. Two works train motor cars ('Tracteurs') brought in a train of flat wagons on which were laid out tables with a sumptuous buffet supper, the sides of the wagons were then let down to form a bridge to the platforms and soon the party was in full swing. Everybody who was anybody came along, and a wonderful time was had by all – the station modernisation programme was thus well and truly launched!

The sixth and final experimental modernisation was carried out at République on line 3 in 1958, and with its orange-coloured panels covering the old tilework, this set the standard for future station modernisation on the Métro. Between 1960 and 1965, therefore, some 73 stations were renovated in a unified style, which allowed greater advertising space than hitherto. The walls were sheeted with metal panels painted a deep creamy-yellow with a green relief. The station seats were an almost continuous bench in either light or dark green or wooden finish, but not surprisingly these seats often attracted those more interested in sleeping than travelling, and in later years, many were

The extensions to the Métro between 1942 and 1952 followed a similar style set hitherto, except for the tiles surrounding names and advertisements, which were less decorative than their predecessors. A block letter 'M' (for Métro) was located in the top centre of each advert display, as seen at Laumiére on 19 April 1950, before the fitting of fluorescent lighting. *RATP*

The first of the 1950s experimental station modernisations was at Franklin D. Roosevelt on line 9, completed in 1952. In 1988 the result was still pleasing, even though bucket seating and 'Tube' TV equipment have been added.

R.J. Greenaway

Modernisation of the line 1 platforms at Franklin D. Roosevelt was completed in 1957, with extensive use made of illuminating glass blocks and advert panels.

R.J. Greenaway

Some 73 stations were modernised in this style between 1960 and 1965, the original tiles being covered by panels. The colour scheme is generally brown and cream/yellow, with light green relief. Several of the stations modernised in this form have been further modernised in a different style, but many survive in some form or another such as at Pont de Neuilly on line 1. *John Thomason*

cut down to form individual seats, while others were replaced. The station names and platform 'Direction' signs were picked out in cream on a brown background and to the eyes of the British, these stations had a distinct touch of Great Western Railway flavouring about them! The station ceilings were either painted yellow, left with white tiling, or, in the case of cut and cover stations, left with the steel girders showing. Unfortunately this modernisation reduced the available platform area and brought about increased problems of cleaning and maintenance of the original tilework behind. For these reasons, the style was abandoned after 1965.

The next style of renovation appeared in 1969, initially at Mouton-Duvernet on line 4, and the opportunity was seized to refurbish stations which most needed attention to tilework. In this scheme, the old white tiles were removed completely and replaced by new flat yellow-orange tiles up to 2.20 metres high on platform side walls. This section of the

République station on line 5 is one of 21 modernised between 1969 and 1974, where yellow/orange tiles replaced the original bevelled white tiles. The platform edge lighting can be appreciated, as well as the deliberate intention to keep the vault in shadow. *R.J. Greenaway*

platform wall, including the advertisement panels, was illuminated, but the main lighting was arranged in shaded 'blocks' along the platform edge. The roof of the station remained in shadow and the overall effect was rather gloomy compared to the previous type. A further variation in station name signs appeared with this style, being white on grey. Most of these have now been replaced by the standard white on blue nameplates and many of the individually-shaped groups of bench seats have been replaced as well. A total of 21 stations were modernised to this design which acquired the style name of 'Mouton-Duvernet' after the prototype. It was realised at an early stage that the finished product was ' . . . not in accord . . . with fashionable ideas'.

In 1973, therefore, a design panel was set up to advise on future station modernisation policy. Its main recommendation was that the vaulted roof of the station should become a focal point of the design, instead of being left in obscurity, and that it should be indirectly lit by sodium lamps. It was also suggested that white should remain as the predominant colour but that the tiles should be relieved by two bands of similar or matching colour, at the level of the seats and on the lighting strip over the edge of the platform. A new type of bucket seating (also in matching colours) was devised to replace the wooden benches and the various items of platform furniture were also regrouped to give an impression of visual unity, making the stations look tidier. Three stations were thus modernised as trials in 1974 and met with an enthusiastic response from the public. The comments made, however, showed that there was still some desire for variety. The three stations chosen for the trials were Pont-Neuf (line 7), Ledru-Rollin (8) and Voltaire (9). In the general application of this scheme, therefore, six colours were chosen not only for variety, but to complement the luminosity of the sodium lighting. The colours used were red, lemon yellow, dark blue, lime green, orange and light brown. The scheme has not been slavishly copied in every instance, but it has been varied where necessary to suit the characteristics of a particular station. At the original cut and cover stations, for instance, the overhead steel girders have been repainted in colours matching the station furniture.

This programme was halted in 1985, following cuts in spending within the RATP, but not before 93 stations had been modernised in this successful style. Many stations have been extensively modernised with completely new flat tiles, while 50 other stations still retain the old bevelled tiles, which have been replaced only where necessary. Some of the latter type of stations still retain tiled station names and original tiled advert surrounds.

Louise Michel on line 3 is one of nearly 100 stations modernised between 1974 and 1985, where the lighting is also used to brighten up the vault. The platform edge lighting, bucket seating and tiled bases are in identical (red) colours. The white bevelled tiles have been replaced by new flat tiles. Near to the platform edge a rough surface has been added, to assist passengers with impaired sighting. *R.J. Greenaway*

Mairie de Montreuil station, the eastern terminus of line 9, under modernisation in 1981 and showing the installation of the platform edge lighting. A train of MF67 stock arrives (left), while a train of Sprague stock (right) awaits departure.
R.J. Greenaway

Cut-and-cover built stations, too, have been modernised based on the 1974 style, but Hôtel de Ville on line 1 incorporates the theme relating to that name. The cross girders are included in the scheme, being painted in the adopted colour of light blue.
John Thomason

Between the various modernisation schemes, a number of experimental styles have been tried. At Odéon (line 10) the platform tiles were removed and the walls were painted in a very pale pink. Station names comprised illuminated signs, red on pale pink. This was done in 1967. Other experiments include Opéra (lines 7 and 8). Havre-Caumartin (line 9) and Saint-Lazare (lines 12 and 13), all five of which were really variations of the Mouton-Duvernet style, done in the same period, 1972-73, but differed in the colour of tiles used. Other stations to follow a similar style to the Mouton-Duvernet group include Gambetta (the new station on line 3), and Kléber, both of which have bevelled fawn-coloured tiles, the two new stations on line 13 (Miromesnil and Champs-Élysées-Clémenceau) and the modernised station at the former on line 9.

Most of the tunnel stations built since the 1970s on the Métro are instantly recognisable as being of cut and cover construction, with their rectangular boxed shape. A good deal of individuality has been shown in the design of these stations, with imagination used for lighting schemes and decoration.

Above **A view of Boulogne-Pont de Saint-Cloud platforms on line 10, showing the rectangular construction, opened in 1981. This is one of a few recently-opened stations with fluorescent lighting hidden by globe shades.**
R.J. Greenaway

The far end of Mairie des Lilas station on line 11 shows both a TV monitor and a reflective mirror for use by the train operator. *R.J. Greenaway*

The reduction in finance available to modernise stations has meant less grandiose products from the mid-1980s, the result being minor renovations, often with small theme displays (q.v. below). The chance has been taken to exploit the 1960–65 style, often by repainting the cream panels white (18 stations so treated by September 1987), and others by utilising and repainting the ducting with a pleasing finish (five stations). In mid-1987 the RATP began a pilot scheme in station modernisation at Stalingrad on line 7. This is a total renovation, but cheaper techniques and materials are being used. In February 1988, much of the work had been completed, but sections of the station are finished in alternative schemes, in trying out various styles of station furniture and lighting for future schemes. Work was also underway with the modernisation of Balard station (line 8) and plans were also advanced for the updating of Réaumur-Sébastopol (4), Montparnasse-Bienvenüe (4 and 12), Saint-Augustin (9), Porte de Pantin (5) and Bastille (1).

In addition to the many variations to station styles on the Métro, the specific themes at selected stations, often incorporated within a particular modernisation scheme, deserve special mention. The first and perhaps most famous station is at Louvre on line 1, so completed in 1968 with replica exhibits from the nearby Louvre Museum, indirectly lit against a restful background of cream-coloured stone, and Saint-Denis-Basilique, commemorating the Royal Basilica of Saint-Denis. A selection of other stations with themes include:

Line 6   MONTPARNASSE-BIENVENÜE – Photographic section on eastbound platform showing development of Métro in honour of Fulgence Bienvenüe, the 'Father of the Métro'.

Line 1   CHAMPS-ÉLYSÉES-CLÉMENCEAU – Science showcases (nearby Musée de la Découverture).

Line 13   VARENNE – This station is near to the Biron Mansion, in which is located the Rodin Museum, housing his sculptures. Replica statues can be seen on the southbound island platform, each piece being spotlit.

Line 3   RÉAUMUR-SÉBASTOPOL – The 'Fleet Street' area of Paris. There are displays in connection with the nearby Press Museum.

Line 8   ECOLE MILITAIRE – Displays relating to the nearby military academy.

Line 2   VICTOR HUGO – Displays commemmorating the work of this famous writer.

Line 3   PARMENTIER – An agricultural theme, with the potato given prominence.

Line 7b   BOLIVAR – A display about the work and life of Simon Bolivar.

Line 13   LIÈGE – Restored to Nord-Sud style, with murals relating to this Belgian city.

Line 10   CLUNY LA SORBONNE – Reopened in February 1988 after being closed for nearly forty years, the station has mosaic tiles on the vault depicting birds and signatures of famous names connected with Sorbonne University.

A recent station modernisation completed in September 1987 was at Parmentier on line 3 which, as can be seen, still retains some of its 1960–65 features. The theme employed here is that of agriculture, more specifically featuring the potato.   *R.J. Greenaway*

It would be wrong to consider the stations of the Métro solely in terms of their interior design and to neglect one of their most characteristic features, the entrances. While the access stairways and passageways, constructed with due regard for economy, were undistinguished and, in many cases, very soon inadequate for the volume of traffic, the CMP, with some prompting from Charles Garnier, decided to make the entrances 'an object of beauty' and to this end organised a competition for their design. As far back as 1886, when it seemed likely that the long-discussed underground railway was about to be built, Garnier, the architect of the Paris Opéra, wrote to the then Minister of Public Works and urged that the Métro should shun all association with industry and turn instead to bronze and stone, marble and triumphal columns, adorned with sculptures. Nothing came of the 1886 project and the art form most closely associated with the Métro was one totally different from Garnier's classicism. None of the designs submitted – all very dependent on traditional ideas – pleased the directors of the CMP and their final choice was rejected by the municipality. The Chairman of the company, the banker Adrien Bernard, who was himself a great admirer of Art Nouveau, then had the inspired idea of awarding the commission to a relatively unknown young architect, Hector Guimard, who was only 32 at the time. Having qualified as an architect and won a travel scholarship, he did not follow the well-trodden path to Rome, but instead went off to Brussels, where he studied under Vincent Horta, the first European exponent of Art Nouveau. Working in forged iron, Guimard created balustrades in which curves and hollows flowed into each other without beginning or end and the letter 'M' was created by their meeting. The entrances were marked by two curving uprights, at the end of which were flower-like globes, illuminted at night. Between these was a plate with the name 'Métropolitain' in flowing letters and the signature of the architect. At the more important stations, the entrances were covered by pavilions in the same general style, but with variations, those at Bastille and Étoile being almost monumental, with a touch of the oriental.

Guimard was not without his critics, and as early as 1904 the CMP was persuaded to abandon the designs he had prepared for Opéra and to substitute rather pedestrian stone balustrades designed by Cassien Bernard. Nevertheless, some 87 Guimard entrances survive on lines 1 to 8, and in 1978 were given the protection of 'listed building' status. Two have also found their way into museums of modern art, in New York and Paris. The pavilions have fared less well and only Porte Dauphine on line 2 survives, blending quietly into the trees of the Bois de Boulogne. None of the canopies remain on their original site, but that from Hôtel de Ville was re-erected at Abbesses when displaced by the entry to an underground car park. While it adds character to the pretty little Montmartre square in which it stands, it is historically quite out of place, as the Nord-Sud at no time availed itself of Guimard's talents.

Apart from the stone balustrades mentioned above, Guimard's style gave way to a much more sombre design in wrought iron, designed by Dervaux. First used on the southern section of line 4, these entrances were generally used for all stations opened between the wars. They are marked by a column surmounted by a globe, illuminated at night. The Nord-Sud used a similar design, but with a more intricate design of balustrade. Reinforced concrete pavilions appeared on the extensions of the 1930s, generally used to provide cover for escalators.

Entrances constructed in recent years have used modern materials such as fibreglass and are generally much lighter and simpler than those of earlier days. Present-day escalators can be unprotected and many exit directly onto the street. A post with a yellow 'M' is a rather plain successor to the Guimard entrances.

Station ticket offices were originally very simple and not particularly inviting. Gradually these became more welcoming. Maps of the system appeared and in 1937 these were supplemented by illuminated journey planners. In 1946 maps of the surrounding area were first displayed (q.v. below) and gradually, where space permitted, other facilities such as news-stands, telephones, information booths and boutiques have been added to make available to passengers a wide range of services.

Within stations, directions are given with reference to the termini of a line – there is no need to carry a compass, but the visitor should memorise the names of the terminal stations! Intermediate stations are normally listed in the corridor or at the stairs giving access to a platform. These show the stations in line order, with interchanges on the right. On the platforms, exit signs are blue and 'correspondance' (interchange) indications, leading to other lines, are orange. If there is more than one exit, plaques on the wall

One of the Guimard entrances at Palais Royal, photographed in 1977.   *R.J. Greenaway*

One of the Guimard station entrance canopies in place at Abbesses on line 12. This came from Hôtel de Ville on line 1 (CMP) and is not of Nord-Sud origin.   *R.J. Greenaway*

helpfully indicate the names of the streets and the house numbers to which each gives access. Ticket halls and some platforms also have a very useful 'Plan du Quartier' which shows the streets and the more important public buildings in the area, and exactly where the station entrances are situated. Since 1986, television screens have appeared on some platforms, either on pedestals or suspended from the ceilings, which normally relay commercial advertising and news bulletins, but can also be used to give details of interruptions to services, diversions, etc. Known as 'Tube', 49 of the busier Métro station platforms had this feature in September 1987. To combat the ever increasing problem of graffiti on stations, most of the electrical cabinets on platforms have been over-painted in a black-grey random maze pattern, first introduced in June 1987 at Bréguet-Sabin station on line 5.

Lifts

Although the original agreement of 1898 specified that the CMP should instal lifts where there was a difference of 12 metres or more between street and platform level, or between the platforms of two corresponding lines, the CMP at first regarded lifts as an expense to be avoided, and the first was not placed in service (at République) until November 1910. Several more lifts were provided for the deeper stations on lines 4 and 7, but at the outbreak of the war in 1914, only seven stations were so equipped. Several more were placed in service when line 10 was opened and the Nord-Sud company could not avoid the provision of lifts at the deeper stations on line 12. However, they have always been relatively uncommon on the Métro and some of the earlier installations have now been replaced by escalators.

The first lifts were hydraulic, but those for lines 4 and 7 were electrically-powered. An unsuccessful return to hydraulic power was made with the lifts for line 10 and these were replaced by escalators. The first automatic lifts were placed in service at Havre-Caumartin on line 9 in 1937 and after 1945 all older lifts were gradually replaced by new ones for this method of operation. The general rate of travel is 3.5m/second.

At the end of 1987 there were 17 lifts in service at 8 Métro stations, the deepest being 28.70m at Buttes-Chaumont on line 7bis. At certain stations, such as Saint Michel, the lifts take passengers directly to and from platform level.

Left One of the 'Tube' television screens at Les Sablons, line 1, which feature news items and advertising. These can be seen at the busier Métro stations either free-standing as shown here or suspended from the station ceiling (see photograph of Pont de Neuilly on page 50). *R.J. Greenaway*

Right Each Métro platform has alarm facilities whereby passengers can talk to the station supervisor and, in emergency, discharge traction current. To the right can be seen part of an equipment cabinet, many of which have been repainted in a stencilled 'maze' pattern to deter and disguise the application of graffiti, first done at Bréguet Sabin station on line 5 in June 1987. *R.J. Greenaway*

Escalators

While the average depth of Métro stations is not so great in comparison with those on London's tube lines, the development of escalators on the system was for many years a very slow process. Nevertheless, since the first practical escalator in the world was used at the Paris Exhibition in 1900, it is perhaps not surprising that escalators first appeared on the Métro before lifts did. The first escalator was installed at Père-Lachaise in 1909, but even by 1923 only seven machines were in service. These early escalators were rather slow (65 steps/minute) and all were of the shunt landing type with passengers having to step off sideways on leaving. They were thus awkward to use, especially for ladies in fashionable tight hobble-skirts.

Escalators of the modern comb type with wooden cleated treads had a speed of 90 steps/minute and were first used at Porte des Lilas in 1924. Again, development was slow and as late as 1966 there were only 87 in service at 50 stations. In general, escalators were installed only where the difference in height was over 4m and even then very often in the ascending direction only. In part, the use of escalators was held back by the automatic (portillon) gates, which closed off the platforms as trains arrived. As these very quickly led to the build-up of a crowd (when closed), escalators could only be used where there was enough space for this crowd to form without blocking off would-be travellers.

As with the control of tickets, it was the coming of the RER which altered matters. A programme drawn up in 1966 provided for the purchase of 200 new escalators, of which 34 were for the Métro. Since then the growth in the number of escalators has been phenomenal, with 405 in use at 185 stations at the end of 1987. This development has been helped by the introduction in1973 of 'compact' escalators with a width overall of only 1.5m (as against the normal 1.7m) and an angle of incline of 35° as opposed to the usual 30°. These do not require to be protected from the weather and at many places, such as bus interchange stations, they lead directly into the open. The first of the weatherproof escalators was commissioned at Place Monge on line 7. Density of passenger flow rather than the depth of a station is now the main factor governing the installation of new escalators. It should be noted that many escalators on the Métro are controlled by photo-electric cells, and are set in motion by the approach of a passenger. If no others come along, the escalator stops again after sufficient time has elapsed for that passenger to have reached the top or bottom. The general speed of escalators on the Métro is now 100 steps/minute. The longest escalator, 22.45m, is at Place des Fêtes on line 7bis and the shortest, at 3.7m, is at Chaussée d'Antin on line 9. Many other recent installations are less than 4m in length.

A pair of escalators at La Motte Picquet on line 6, which are of the older type, having wooden cleated step treads.
John Thomason

The following list of lines and numbers of escalators (a total of 405 at 185 stations) is as at the end of 1987. It should be pointed out, however, that in some cases the escalators for an interchange station may not necessarily be divided between all the lines served by it – for example, Saint-Lazare (lines 3, 12 and 13) has five serving line 3, ten serving line 13, but none allocated to line 12.

	Escalators	Stations		Escalators	Stations
Line 1	41	13	Line 7bis	6	3
Line 2	15	8	Line 8	32	20
Line 3	49	19	Line 9	42	22
Line 3bis	6	1	Line 10	8	7
Line 4	35	13	Line 11	11	7
Line 5	27	8	Line 12	23	17
Line 6	17	8	Line 13	34	15
Line 7	59	24			

Travolators

Despite the initial planning of the Métro system, it was not always possible to ensure that the distances at interchange stations were as short as the public might have wished and some of the corridors on the Métro are exceptionally long. The CMP had considered the idea of travolators in the 1930s, but had been unable to put the idea into practice beyond ensuring that the necessary width was left in some passageways of new construction. It was not until 1964 that the first pair of travolators were put into service on 21 October at Châtelet, linking lines 1 and 4 with 7 and 11. They were 131m long and 0.92m wide and a speed of 45m/minute (2.7 km/h) allowed them to carry 10,000 passengers per hour. In service they proved to be slightly too small and slow, and when the next set (of three) were installed at Montparnasse-Bienvenüe on 25 July 1968, they were made rather wider (1.12m) and had a speed of 3km/h, allowing a capacity of 11,000 passengers per hour. One single travolator has also been installed at Invalides, connecting the Métro with RER line C, which is operated wholly by the SNCF. The total number of travolators on the Métro is thus six, at three stations.

Station Names

When Baron Haussmann, Préfect of the Seine, drove 85 miles of new streets across Paris between 1855 and 1870, he obliterated many of the ancient villages, so that when the first line of the Métro opened in July 1900, there were few old villages to use for station names. Instead, the names of important buildings on the line of route were used, as well as the name of a Square (Place) or a street (rue), mostly at right-angles to the line. It seems that some of the names had the 'Place de' and 'Rue de' prefixes dropped before signs were installed at stations, apart from a few odd exceptions, which still survive (e.g. Place de Clichy and Rue Montmartre, which are to avoid confusion with Porte de Clichy and Boulevard de Montmartre respectively). With Métro stations spaced close together, names used had to be those of streets where the stations actually were. But as the system grew, the name of a street at right-angles to the first line could be parallel to the second

The impressive triple-bank travolators at Montparnasse-Bienvenüe, opened in 1968 to give easier interchange access between lines 6/13 and 4/12. *John Thomason*

line, for which it was clearly imprecise. In many cases, therefore, a second name was added for the interchange, but in others an entirely new name was used. At the ends of the lines, at the City boundaries, the prefix 'Porte' (Gate) was used on station names, and have been retained, even though the City fortifications had been dismantled by 1920.

Considering France's history, generals and battles of the Napoleons are well represented in station names. There are 18 generals and 5 battles associated with Napoleon I, 5 generals and 4 battles associated with Napoleon III and 7 generals and 9 battles for the rest of French history. Such examples are Cambronne (line 6), Daumesnil (6/8), Duroc (12/13), Kléber (6), Mouton-Duvernet (4) and Pelleport (3bis) – all generals, and Austerlitz (line 5), Pyramides (7), Iéna (9) and Wagram (3) – all battles of Napoleon I.

Double-barrelled names are not always of two streets at right-angles. There are innumerable combinations, but apart from double names in their own right, such as Buttes-Chaumont or Chardon-Lagache, these can be what is in effect one street at right-angles, but which changes its name as it crosses the line, or a street name combined with a square, or a square or bridge combined with a district, or two villages. As there is a flat fare on the Métro, and thus there is no need to ask for specific destination names when purchasing a ticket, passengers do not have to quote some very long names – e.g. 'Boulogne – Pont de Saint-Cloud – Rhin et Danube' on line 10, or 'Bobigny – Pablo Picasso – Préfecture Hôtel du Département' on line 5!

Name changes have, of course, taken place for various reasons. Apart from new lines which have caused name changes to interchange stations, the two world wars have also had their effects on Métro station names. For example, Berlin (Nord-Sud line B, now line 13) was closed in 1914 and later reopened as Liège. In the same year, Allemagne was swiftly renamed Jaurès, after a Socialist politician who had been assassinated in that year. During the First World War, Pont d'Austerlitz became Quai de la Rapée in 1916, and after that war Alma was renamed George V.

After the Second World War, Franklin D. Roosevelt gave his name to a station in 1946 and seven stations were renamed after heroes of the resistance, including the two Corentins (Celton and Cariou) and Colonel Fabien.

In 1942 there were three big changes to give double-barrelled names to stations which had been hitherto linked as interchanges, but under separate names. Montparnasse (line 4 and 12) and Bienvenüe (lines 6 and 14) became Montparnasse-Bienvenüe, which still survives, but the other two have been changed again to become Franklin D. Roosevelt and Stalingrad, both in 1946.

Some names have disappeared from the map, only to re-appear elsewhere at a later date. These include Rue Saint-Denis which became Réaumur-Sébastopol in 1907, the first year of any name changes on the Métro, but was used in Boulevard Saint-Denis opened on line 4 in 1908, and by line 13 reaching the actual town of Saint-Denis in 1976. Austerlitz, disappearing in 1916, re-appeared as Gare d'Orléans-Austerlitz in 1930. Today, it is just plain Gare d'Austerlitz, even though the destinations of some trains on line 10 still refer to the previous name, from which it was renamed in 1977. Already mentioned is that Alma became George V in 1920, but Alma-Marceau opened in 1923. Torcy became Marx Dormoy in 1946, but re-appeared as a New Town at the end of the new branch on RER line A in 1980. Line 4's station at Vaugirard was renamed Saint Placide in 1913, three years after the Nord-Sud company's Vaugirard station with the same name was opened – and remains so named to this day. In addition, the name Sèvres appears twice on the Métro – in Pont de Sèvres (line 9) and Sèvres-Babylone (lines 10 and 12).

Recent renamings of Métro stations have been relatively few. In 1970 Bagnolet became Alexandre Dumas, with Porte de Bagnolet being used on a new extension on line 3 the following year. Also in 1970 Étoile became Charles de Gaulle - Étoile after the famous Statesman. In 1986 the line 9 platforms at Nation were renamed Nation - Place des Antilles, the Antilles being the French Overseas Département in the West Indian archipelago.

In addition to all the main station names, there are many which have suffixes in their own right. For example, Javel - André Citroën (the latter in respect of the famous car manufacturer) and Porte d'Orléans - Général Leclerc, the suffix honouring the famous Free French General, who entered Paris at the head of his armoured division, and liberated Strasbourg. He was posthumously promoted 'Marshal' in 1952, so that the street and station names are technically incorrect. Another World War II hero is honoured in Porte Dauphine - Maréchal de Lattre de Tassigny.

CHAPTER 5
ROLLING STOCK

The Original Trains

The original rolling stock of the CMP had a distinct affinity with contemporary tramcars. The wooden-bodied cars were about 8m long and carried at most 50 passengers. They rode on four-wheel trucks and had two 125 hp motors. Air brakes were used. For their size they were very heavy, the motor coaches weighing 18.5 tonnes and the trailers 8.5 tonnes. Two single-width sliding doors were originally provided on each side, one for entry and one for exit, but in a very short time these were seen to be inadequate, and after 1902 new deliveries had double-width doors, the earlier cars being converted to this design. Twelve of the original motor coaches were double-ended but the majority had only one driving cab. Because of the events related below, the two-axle motors had a very short life and all had been withdrawn by 1906. The trailers were in some cases rebuilt as bogie motors but others survived unaltered on lines 2 and 6 until 1932.

The first trains on line 1 consisted of a motor coach pulling two trailers, but this formation very soon became insufficient to cope with the traffic and in 1901 it was decided to strengthen these and to operate trains of seven or eight coaches on line 2. As multiple unit traction was then in its infancy, there was no certainty that it would be able to cope with the demands of everyday traffic on the Métro and it was therefore decided to adopt the Thomson 'double traction' system, which had been devised in 1898 and which, though somewhat limited in its ultimate potential, was both simple and robust. Current collection and control was by the leading motor coach. Current was passed through a huge controller to the motors of both the leading and another motor coach at line voltage by a bus line and, as the CMP placed the second motor at the rear on lines without terminal loops, this line ran the length of the train. When accelerating, resistances were not cut out progressively as in normal systems, but were instead brought in in parallel with the resistance on the previous notch of the controller and it was not possible to bridge the gap from series to parallel operation without briefly cutting off the current. This manœuvre demanded care on the part of the driver, since the slightest backward movement of the controller could produce arcing. The equipment was protected by circuit breakers, not seen again on the Métro until the advent of the articulated stock (MA52) in 1952. The power-weight ratio on an eight-coach train was very low (500hp to approximately 110 tonnes with a full load) and the little motor coaches were often seen to be labouring on the ramps leading to the elevated sections of line 2. But the double-traction trains had solved the capacity problem and an order for 284 additional vehicles was placed in 1903.

On 10 August 1903 a short-circuit caused a fire to break out in the leading motor coach of a double-traction train at Boulevard Barbès station just at the end of the evening rush hour. The staff on the spot decided to push the train to the siding at Belleville by using the following four-coach train, both trains being emptied of their exasperated passengers. Despite warnings by large clouds of black smoke issuing from the disabled motor, the convoy set off. Unfortunately the points at Belleville had not been set for the siding and it was decided to press on to the terminus at Nation, the train by now being in tunnel. It had reached Ménilmontant when fire broke out with terrible strength. At that moment, the following very crowded train stopped in Couronnes, the preceding station, and the Station Master, with great promptitude, asked the passengers to evacuate the train, but the majority stayed put until the cloud of smoke issued from the tunnel mouth and all the lights went out. Loss of life was considerable – 84 passengers perished in this disaster. Not only the CMP, but underground railways generally, learned much from it.

There were many factors contributing to the disaster, but the immediate blame was placed on the underpowered, wooden motor coaches and the order just placed was cancelled. As a temporary measure, the maximum train length was reduced to seven coaches, with the two motors placed together at the head, but as soon as was practicable they were withdrawn for conversion to bogie stock, the last running on 14 May 1906.

The Classic Stock

The history of the Classic, Sprague, stock is extremely complicated and as it is almost extinct, no more than a summary can be attempted here.

The first two prototype bogie motor coaches were delivered in December 1902 and April 1903 and were numbered 1001 and 1002. They had wooden bodies but the driving compartments and switchgear were encased in metal. They worked as a double-traction unit and spent all of their lives on line 2, later being renumbered 301/2. Briefly in 1914-15 they were re-equipped with four motors, but the experiment was not successful and they were re-converted to two-motor condition. These vehicles, however, set the general standard of appearance for all stock built up to 1937.

Even before the Couronnes fire, the CMP seemed to have been considering the use of multiple-unit control, probably recognising that the double-traction equipment could only be a stop-gap. An eight-coach train, with three two-axle motor coaches working in multiple-unit, appeared on line 1 early in November 1903, and so anxious was the CMP to see how it would perform, that it was apparently placed in service before official permission to use it had been given. This train used the Sprague system, one of three then available. Wisely, the CMP spent much time and money evaluating the various systems, both singly and in combination, before finally deciding in 1908 on the Sprague-Thomson system. It was an excellent choice and was to give superb service for 75 years, standing up uncomplainingly to the overcrowding and minimal maintenance of the years of the second world war.

The Sprague system of multiple unit operation, already in use on the Chemin de Fer de l'Ouest, consisted of an electro-magnetic reverser and a pilot-motor-operated drum controller. Current relays gave automatic acceleration and only five control wires were used. The system was essentially simple and easy to maintain, but it tended to be imprecise and jerky in operation, especially in the transition from series to parallel.

The Westinghouse system was electro-pneumatic, using a control line of seven wires and contactors. It required frequent and careful maintenance and even then it was not always possible to ensure that the same amount of current reached each motor at the same time. Acceleration was slow and, with an inexperienced driver, could be jerky. By the 1920s, when the 100 Westinghouse motors were concentrated on line 4, the equipment was wearing out and chaos often ensued when second-time exasperated passengers abandoned trains which had stalled on the climb to Gare du Nord, making it necessary to cut off the current to prevent a major tragedy. By the time normality was restored in the late evening, trains were completely out of order and the railway management in despair! The Westinghouse trains were withdrawn in 1929/30 and converted to Sprague-Thomson equipment. This conversion would have taken place earlier if finance had been available. The problems caused by the Westinghouse trains put the CMP off anything electro-pneumatic until the advent of the rubber-tyred trains in the 1950s.

Of the three systems available, the Thomson control proved to be the best. It allowed both hand notching or automatic acceleration, the latter being activated by the handle of the master controller through a spring-operated drum. It gave precise control of each motor in a train (though all worked at the pace of the weakest), it was easy to maintain and it was reliable. The main drawback was that the control line required nine wires and it was impossible to add supplementary notches to the complex and rather delicate control mechanism. It had reached the limit of its development, and was fitted to 271 coaches.

Having experimented and gained some experience of each of these forms of control, the CMP decided to adopt a combination of the Sprague and Thomson systems. In this Sprague-Thomson system, a small master controller energised one or more of a small number of train wires commanding self-contained automatic electro-magnetic contactor equipment. This gave easy and smooth control of acceleration and also allowed the grouping of motors so that failure of one did not incapacitate an entire train. Following experiments, the first trains so equipped were placed in service in 1908. From then until the 1930s, the Sprague-Thomson system gradually replaced all other forms of control and gave the CMP a secure and reliable fleet, with a degree of standardisation not enjoyed by any other operator before or since. The only later exception was a batch of 21 motor coaches with Jeumont-Heidmann equipment delivered in 1930. Although this gave excellent results on the gradients of line 3, the interest of standardisation prevailed and no more such equipment was purchased for the Métro. These trains could not be worked with Sprague-Thomson stock. This type of equipment was later used on the Chemin de Fer d'Orléans stock, more familiarly known as the Z stock of the Ligne de Sceaux.

Following the successful operation of the prototypes and as a result of the Couronnes fire, the CMP placed 177 motor bogie coaches in service in 1904 and 1905. Before they entered service, however, the train of four-wheelers fitted with Sprague multiple unit equipment had been tried in November 1903 on line 1. The bogie coaches carried these experiments a stage further. They were of two lengths; the 300 class were only 10.85m long and had two doors per side, while the 400 class had an additional area for standing passengers immediately behind the compartment housing the equipment. Some of the former had double-traction control and went to line 2, but the majority were fitted for multiple-unit operation and went to line 1. All the 400 class were m.u. fitted and were placed in service on line 3. All the 300 class m.u. motor cars were lengthened in 1910 to make them identical with the 400 class and both of these classes received four motors in 1929-32, surviving unchanged until withdrawal from the late-1960s and into the 1970s. The double traction members of the 300 class were withdrawn in 1931 and many of the parts were used in the building of new four-motor coaches.

The next series to appear were 114 rebuilds of four-wheel motors, those with Westinghouse equipment being fitted for multiple unit operation, using the products of the same manufacturer, while the double-traction coaches retained this equipment. As rebuilt, they were identical to the 300 class. In 1906-07, 56 two-axle cars were similarly rebuilt and finally another batch of 24 were built new. This last batch were the first coaches on the Métro to have all-metal bodywork. The majority of these coaches were lengthened in 1909-12 so that they also resembled the 400 class and a large number were further rebuilt with four motors between 1929 and 1936, in the course of which operation the remaining wooden bodies were replaced by metal ones. Those built for service on line 1 were in grey livery.

The grey-liveried Sprague stock could always be found on line 1 until displaced by 'pneu' stock in 1963–64, when it then went to line 8, and in its final years to lines 12, 2 and 9. M474 was scrapped as recently as April 1987, having been stored out of use since July 1981. It is seen on the connection between lines 9 and 10 near to the never-opened station of Porte Molitor.
R.J. Greenaway

The next batch of new coaches, the 500s, reverted to the longer length of the 400 class, but had all-metal bodywork. Their history was much less complicated since they were not rebuilt in any way and the class survived intact until after 1967. These were the first to have Sprague-Thomson equipment and so may be regarded as the definitive version of the Classic stock. They were followed in 1909 by the broadly similar 600 class which, however, originally had Thomson equipment, and in 1913-14 by the 700 class, which had Sprague-Thomson and incorporated various minor improvements. The last of these were intended for line 6 and would have had two driving cabs, but because of the German advance into northern France in 1914 they were never built.

The motor coaches delivered after the First World War were characterised by a much smaller switchgear compartment, with a consequent enlargement of the passenger area. This series appeared between 1921 and 1927 and the last 18 were double-ended for use on line 10 and the shuttle (Navette).

To improve service speeds on the busier lines, it was decided in 1925 to introduce four-motored motor coaches of a slightly greater length. The first batch of 62, 14.2m long, had three pairs of doors per side and went into service in 1927-28, mostly on line 3, but some migrated to line 12 after the merger of the Nord-Sud company with the CMP. Of the later deliveries, all were of the same length and all had four pairs of double doors per side. About half were built new and the rest were rebuilds of earlier stock (q.v. above). Ten of the new coaches were in grey livery. The four-motor stock could always be distinguished by a small signalling window to the right of the driving cab. The last batches of four-motor cars had the arrangement of the doors and windows equally spaced on each side.

The Nord-Sud motor coaches did not differ greatly from their contemporaries on the CMP and although built over the period 1909-25, were all visually identical to each other. They were slightly larger in profile and heavier than the Métro stock and had a much improved design of bogie. As they had less powerful motors, their progress was comfortable and stately rather than lively! Apart from one coach scrapped as a result of an accident just after the Nord-Sud merger with the CMP, all were incorporated into CMP stock in 1930. One coach was damaged by bombing in 1944 and, with eight others, was rebuilt for works train duties in 1952, but all the others survived in service until 1971-72. The increase in line voltage was the main reason for their rather sudden demise.

Nord-Sud motor car M90, seen in Vaugirard depot in 1934, four years after takeover by the CMP and in renumbered form – M2090. The photograph shows the overhead pantograph in position, this system being abandoned on lines 12 and 13 in 1931, although retained for depot shunting until 1952. *RATP*

The Nord-Sud stock was displaced from line 13 by the articulated stock in 1952–53, but survived on line 12 until 1972. A farewell run on 12 May 1972 pauses at Madeleine.   *RATP*

The first bogie trailer cars were delivered with the 400 class motors, which they closely resembled, though the first class vehicles were panelled in metal and were thus the first coaches on the Métro to be painted rather than varnished. The next batch were shorter and were intended to make up, with corresponding motors, six-coach trains on line 1. They later went to other lines and when withdrawn in 1935 three were sold to the Brussels-Tervuren Electric Railway, for which they had to be re-gauged. This is the only case of Métro stock being sold for further service on urban railways elsewhere. These were followed in the period 1908-13 by a large number of trailers based on the 500 class motors. After the First World War came two batches of trailers 13.60m long of which eight, fitted with Brill diamond bogies, were by far the most comfortable of all Métro coaches. Unfortunately the experiment was not repeated. Finally, there were five lots of four-door trailers, corresponding to the four-motor motor coaches. Many of these were painted grey for line 1 and in these rather more attention was paid to detail than was generally the case. The last batch had lightweight aluminium bodies and a new design of bogie, and weighed only 15.2 tonnes.

The Nord-Sud trailers resembled very closely that system's motor cars, but were fitted with rectangular end windows.

The interior of all varieties of the Classic stock was simple to the point of austerity. The seats in the second class were of painted or varnished wood, while the first class boasted leather upholstery, but without a great deal of padding. Lighting was by three strings of 5×40W lamps and ventilation was provided by drop windows (on one side of the coach only, to prevent cross-draughts) and by wide open vents in the lantern roof. Some of the

The interior of the Sprague stock was always pretty basic, with wooden slatted seats, open lantern ventilation and pull-down windows on one side only. Note the elaborate stove enamel panelling and the 'CMP' monogram on the cab door in the background.   *RATP*

The last line to operate Sprague stock trains was line 9 in 1983, which culminated in a week of official RATP farewell celebrations. In March 1981, M355 heads a train at Miromesnil. The small observance window to the left of the driver's window can be seen, as can the guard at the leading pair of doors.
R.J. Greenaway

The complete Sprague stock fleet all had a similar appearance, but there were many minor detail variations between the numerous batches. M222 at Choisy depot shows that the destination plate position is over the driver's window. This car started life in 1902, being rebuilt in 1905 and 1912, assuming its final form in 1931. It survived until 1976, when it was scrapped.   *RATP*

last coaches to be built also had ventilators at foot level and travel on these on the open section of lines 2 and 6 in winter was guaranteed to chill even the most devoted rail fan, let alone the ordinary passengers. Neither heating nor sound insulation was provided and the train noises were thus most enjoyable for the enthusiast, though probably less so for the uninitiated. The floors, of corrugated sheet steel, were covered with magnesium cement.

The driving cabs were simply equipped, the driver sitting (but more often standing) on the right, working the controller with his right hand and the air brake valve with his left. The only instrument provided was the air-brake pressure gauge and speed had to be estimated. Glazed doors and panels gave the passenger a good view of all this, as well as of the fireworks from the traction-line switches, which were mounted, without any covering, to the left of the cab. There was no deadman's handle, but the master controller sprang back to 'off' if released and could not be moved away from that position unless the button in the centre of the handle was first depressed. In any case, the guard travelled in the leading coach at the leading pair of doors and was within sight of the driver.

The bogies were of 2.25m wheelbase and were of two types. Those built before 1912 had simple springing while the newer ones had a swing bolster. In neither case was the ride especially comfortable. Trailer bogies were of 1.8m wheelbase. The Westinghouse air brake was unsophisticated, with one cylinder per coach acting on one or two brake blocks per wheel. To prevent the deposition of metallic dust in the tunnels the brake blocks were of copper beech drenched in vegetable oil, giving off the typical Sprague era 'perfume'. The compressors were situated under the floor on motor coaches.

The Classic stock not only set the visual aspect of the Métro for many years, it also brought many unique sounds and smells, and the system no longer seems the same without it!

The last of the two-motored Sprague stock was withdrawn from service on line 2 in 1976, M899 seen at Nation on 16 March 1976 being in the final formation. *RATP*

The original livery of the Classic stock was varnished wood and when the first all-metal coaches appeared, they were painted dark brown to match. Later, this was changed to a dark ('olive') green and in the 1920s this was in turn replaced by a medium green. The grey stock for line 1 was officially grey-blue, but the blue generally had to be imagined, as it faded very quickly. Many of the rebuilt coaches still incorporated the brown wooden doors of the original stock. The Nord-Sud stock was a pleasing shade of royal blue, with the first class trailers being cream with red ends. The CMP first class trailers were at first denoted by two white boards carried below the waist rail, but when the green livery was adopted for second class, first class trailers became red.

By 1937, therefore, the CMP had at its disposal a highly-standardised fleet. Apart from the coaches with J-H equipment, all stock had identical control, although the ex-Nord-Sud stock could not be coupled in multiple with the CMP stock. This standardisation and the rugged simplicity of the Classic stock were a godsend to both the maintenance and traffic staff during the difficult war years, when the Métro had to cope with unprecedented loads, but in time these very virtues became a drawback. As the standards of public expectation rose in the post-war period, the Métro began to seem noisy, uncomfortable and antiquated – it did not help that the trains built as recently as 1937 were really themselves based on designs dating back to 1903! The few experiments that were made, such as those with fluorescent lighting and regenerative braking, were isolated examples, intended to try out new ideas for the next generation of rolling stock, rather than to improve the Classic stock itself.

By any standards, the Classic stock of the Métro had an extraordinarily long career, spanning as it did the 79 years 1904–1983. Apart from two cars destroyed in the war (M33 and Bb619), systematic withdrawal of the Classic stock began only with the conversion of line 1 to 'pneu' operation, but even then many trains were transferred to reinforce other lines rather than being sent to the scrapyard. It was only when the MF67 stock began to arrive that serious inroads were made in the ranks of Sprague trains, which disappeared from lines 3 and 7 in 1971 and 1973 respectively. Some of these trains in due course turned up to replace the Nord-Sud stock on line 12. The extension of line 8 also created a need for many more trains and gave the Sprague stock a chance to show its paces on the Créteil line, where the stations are more widely spaced than elsewhere. In the 1970s, Sprague stock gave way to 'pneu' trains on line 6 in 1974 and to the articulated stock on line 10 (1975-76), while the last of the two-motor coaches went from line 2 (being replaced by four-motor coaches) in 1976. With the arrival of the MF77 stock, and by transfers of other modern stock, the Sprague stock disappeared from lines 5, 7bis, 8 and 12 in 1980, and from lines 2 and 3bis in 1981. By 1982, only 16 trains remained at work on line 9. These would have gone in September, but the flooding at Eglise de Pantin on 6 June 1982 and the subsequent temporary withdrawal of 18 MF67 trains granted a stay of execution, so that the last Sprague trains were finally withdrawn in April 1983.

However, they did not simply fade away. The Parisians had by now realised that a part of their city's history was about to pass away and the RATP commemorated the event with a ceremony never before accorded to any underground train. Under the general title of 'Salut l'Artiste', a series of events took place between 11 and 16 April 1983. At Miromesnil station there were, on successive days, a film show, a children's party, a mannequin parade and a concert, all in addition to a computer display. Saint-Augustin station hosted an exhibition on 'Art and the Métro' on the wide eastbound platform, while a rake of Sprague stock was stationed in the bay platform at Concorde on line 8, some of the carriages converted into a boutique selling souvenirs. Meanwhile, four Sprague trains (three of them decorated with special themes) ran to a published timetable on line 9 in the midday period, to cater for those who wanted a last ride. On Friday 15 April there was the official RATP farewell, when three trains carried official dignitaries from Porte de Montreuil to Pont de Sèvres and into Boulogne depot. After 79 years, therefore, it was (almost) over, with the very last public runs taking place on Saturday 16 April. It had been a worthy end to a great career.

In fact, the last trains with the official party did not mark the end of the Sprague stock, which, in one form or another, will be around for some time yet. There are, for example, the official museum pieces at Saint Mandé (nearest station, Porte Dorée on line 8), plus others stored at Invalides intended for the Museum, but other coaches survive, preserved elsewhere, both in the French provinces and abroad. Three complete operational trains have been retained by the RATP for use in film making and on enthusiasts' specials – Sprague stock has starred in many films, as in a hair-raising scene in 'Diva', where the young hero rides his motor scooter down a stairway and into a Sprague train!

Nord-Sud motor coach M102 (CMP M2102) was one of the last batch to be built in 1925 by SFB, now preserved in the Transport Museum at Saint Mandé.   *Brian Patton*

Depot shunting motor TA01 at Choisy in September 1987 in yellow livery was originally Sprague motor car M340.   *Brian Hardy*

Other survivors have had less glamorous roles. Many have been converted to 'Tracteurs' (works train motor cars) for engineering trains, the majority of post-war conversions being double-ended, two-motor coaches (less the trailing ends) making one Tracteur. Early works motor cars included the double-ended wooden four-wheel motors (MM1-12), displaced from passenger train duties in 1906, and lasting until 1949. Early conversions began in 1922 with T1 and T2 (originally being M313 and M316), followed by a further 29 done in the period 1928–37. There are also a small number of Sprague motor coaches in use to transfer stock between depots. These are known as 'Tracteurs Ateliers' (depot motors) and, like the works train Tracteurs, are fitted with both conventional and 'pneu' system shoegear, to enable them to work on all lines. Many trailers have been converted over the years into various wagons, which bear the prefix 'V' or 'VX'. A small number of trailers retain their bodywork and are used as Personnel Carriers for works train staff. Other Sprague cars retained but not absorbed in the service stock fleet have included mobile classrooms (looking especially smart in the blue and white livery of the MF67 stock), and a car used for demonstrating the re-railing of derailed trains.

Amid all the 'Sprague Mania' that swept Paris in April 1983, the only sour note was struck by the (then) Minister of Transport, who characterised the Classic trains as uncomfortable, noisy and slow. He was wrong on the last point – Sprague trains may be slow to accelerate, but given a clear road, can develop a fair speed – but nobody could contradict him on the other points. So why did so many people, the majority not railway enthusiasts, turn out to mark their passing?

For the passengers, it was probably the sense of permanence imparted by the 'square' green or grey trains that mattered most. Wars, depression, civil commotion, occupation, austerity and General de Gaulle came and went in turn and the Sprague trains just kept on running – and running – taking children to school, commuters to work, lovers to rendezvous, old folk to visit each other and tourists everywhere. To these last, the Eiffel Tower and Sprague trains were Paris. By the 1970s, only the very old could remember Paris without the Classic trains. They were part of everyone's childhood and when they went, people began to realise that they, too, were growing old. And for those who had lived through the years of the occupation, when the buses vanished from the streets, it was often the Métro that got them home by curfew.

The staff saw the Classic stock in many different ways. To the workshops the Sprague-Thomson trains were superb – they needed minimal maintenance and they just kept running, even under the abuse of wartime loadings. To the driver of a two-motor coach, perched on a small wooden stool, his knees wedged between the controller and the brake valve and sweating in a temperature of 40°, they were far from ideal. The older motors lacked adhesion and, when the autumn leaves fluttered down onto the tracks of line 2, many a train stalled on the ramp up to the viaduct and had to wait a push from a 'Tracteur'. Sometimes they also lacked braking force – coming down from Gare de l'Est on line 4 in the evening rush hour, a driver could find that, despite the continual thumping of the compressor, he would become short of air and be pushed into the tunnel by the sheer weight of humanity aboard. Or on line 1, especially in the days of two-motor trains, a driver could never be sure that he would make it up the ramp and round the curve into Bastille. And all this against an incessant barrage of clacking from the contactors and sparking from the switchgear, in a very confined space. There was no speedometer – speeds were estimated and, if making up time after a prolonged station stop, one prayed that no inspector was hiding in a niche in the tunnel, stopwatch in hand.

And yet the Sprague trains gave to the men who worked them a comradeship and a sense of craft denied to those who knew only the modern stock. A driver had to respect both his conducteur and the limitations of his train. In the absence of a speedometer, the sound of the contactors and the crescendo of the motors were a good indication of progress – but first the notes of the 'music' had to be learned. A knowledge of the geography of the system helped and even the slightest downgrade could allow a driver to regain a few precious seconds after a delay – the real expert could profit by this without catching up with the train in front. Given all that, one could be fairly certain that the Sprague stock would get to the destination on time. And, if the worst happened and there was a failure, the chances were that repairs could be made on the spot, in a matter of minutes. And at the end of the month there was a bonus for the driver who had been most economical in the use of current. The man who went home with that had really won his spurs – he knew his Sprague trains AND he knew his Métro.

There were numerous batches of Sprague stock, of all types of cars, each one ultimately representing one small piece of a very large jigsaw puzzle. Many different car builders were involved over the years in making the Classic stock, which, at its maximum in 1937, amounted to 2,720 cars, summarised as follows:

Driving Motor Cars ('M')	CMP M4 (Rebuilds)	340	
	CMP M4 (New Cars)	257	
	CMP M2	626	
	NS M4	114	1337
First Class Trailers ('Ab')	CMP	348	
	NS	51	399
Second Class Trailers ('Bb')	CMP	682	
	NS	100	782
Composite Trailers ('AB')	CMP	202	202
			2720

Remaining Sprague Stock and Locations as at 1 June 1988

M1269	Porte Molitor	Bb578	Choisy depot	Ab1036*	Auteuil depot
M2103*	Auteuil depot	Bb654	Choisy depot	Ab1037*	Auteuil depot
M2104*	Auteuil depot	Bb691	Javel depot		

The operative Sprague trains (for specials, filming, etc.) are located at Monge, and are formed as follows:

M103 —Bb572—Ab487—Bb751—M1350
M333 —Bb761—Ab475—Bb434—M1266
M1308—Bb713—Ab411—Bb782—M429

To be scrapped:

M1218	Daumesnil	Bb474	Daumesnil	Ab467	Daumesnil
M1229	Daumesnil			AB5251	Pré-Saint-Gervais
M1277	Vaugirard depot			AB5337	Daumesnil

Intended Preservation by Paris Transport Museum (AMTUIR):

T13	Porte Molitor	Bb171	Invalides	Ab167	Invalides
M270	Invalides	Bb240	Invalides	Ab253	Invalides
M757	Invalides	Bb546	Invalides	Ab284	Invalides
M857	Invalides			Ab464	Invalides
M1079	Invalides				
M1231	Invalides			AB5338	Invalides

Intended Preservation for Mulhouse Museum:

M1354   Fontenay depot

Intended Private Preservation:

M450	Pré-Saint-Gervais	Bb453	Porte Molitor	AB5205	Porte Molitor
M473	Porte Molitor	Bb549	Porte Molitor		
M1322	Porte Molitor				

*Nord-Sud stock

A five car train of Sprague stock on line 9 at Nation, heading to the eastern terminus of Mairie de Montreuil. The darkness of the station vault highlights the open lantern roofs common to these trains. *R.J. Greenaway*

Two Sprague trains at Mairie de Montreuil in 1981, during the time that the station was being modernised. The construction of the fluorescent lighting at the platform edge can be seen. Note the pistons for the air doors, located on the outside of the cars! *R.J. Greenaway*

The Articulated (MA52) Stock

After the end of the Second World War, studies were instituted for new rolling stock which, by virtue of improved acceleration and braking, would improve overall service speed and thus increase line capacity. These studies ultimately resulted in the articulated trains, the first of which arrived in September 1951 and went into service on line 13 in February 1952. The impending extension of this line from Porte de Saint-Ouen to Carrefour Pleyel (opened on 30 June 1952) made an increase in line capacity imperative.

The car bodies were built by Brissonneau et Lotz and each semi-permanently coupled unit consists of three car bodies resting on four bogies. The outer cars of a unit are 12.70m long and the middle trailer is shorter, at 9.70m. The outer (motor) cars were second class only, while the middle car was a composite. These trains introduced a new colour scheme of light blue and grey for second class and cream with blue lining for first class. Internally, the new stock represented a great step forward, having upholstered seating in both classes, fluorescent lighting, improved ventilation and double doors pneumatically opened when a passenger lifted a latch. Each unit has four self-ventilated motors of 92hp controlled by type JH servo-motor-operated cam-contactor controllers. The bogies are of welded construction and incorporate 'Athermos' axle boxes with radial movement. Most of the bogies were constructed by Alsthom, but in three units by BL (E036, 039 and 040). On the articulated parts, rubber 'Silentblocs' are used. Braking is by Westinghouse air brakes and brake release is done electro-pneumatically under the control of a decelerometer, to give adequate retardation without wheelslip. The trains are fitted with Scharfenberg automatic couplers at the driving ends, but are semi-permanently coupled within units.

In service, the MA52 stock did much of what was expected of it, especially with regard to acceleration, but it was noisy and rough riding and the design was not repeated. Nevertheless, these trains have given sound service for over 35 years, at first on line 13, and since 1975-76 on line 10. Their interior furnishings set a standard which lasted until the MF77 stock appeared.

The MA52 articulated stock is fast approaching the end of its life and the first units were stored from mid-1987. Motor car D67 of unit 034 is seen at the western end of line 10, Boulogne – Pont de Saint-Cloud, opened in October 1981.
R.J. Greenaway

Compared with the interior of Sprague stock, the MA52 was a great improvement. The continuous fluorescent lighting, ventilation slats above it and the tip-up seats were features added with the 1975–76 modernisation programme.
R.J. Greenaway

With line 13 being a 'Y'-shaped line, the articulated MA52 stock was ideal for uncoupling and operating short (one-unit) trains in service at certain off peak times. However, uncoupling ceased in 1972, not only with the stock's imminent transfer to line 10, but also to eliminate the operating problems associated with uncoupling and the extra staff needed for it.

Although given unit numbers, the articulated stock also has individual car numbers, driving motors prefixed 'D' and the shorter middle trailers prefixed 'C', as follows:

Unit	Formation
E001	D01 – C01 – D02
E002	D03 – C02 – D04
and so on, up to:	
E040	D79 – C40 – D80

For service on line 10, the opportunity was taken to modernise the 40 units of the MA52 fleet. A prototype conversion was undertaken at Vaugirard depot from August 1974, being completed in March 1975, unit E030 being the chosen one. The work involved utilising noise-reducing materials, increasing the fluorescent lighting, and installing tip-up seats at all door positions. The exteriors were repainted in a royal blue and white livery with a dark blue waistband, the first class section being denoted by a yellow band at cantrail height. The modernisation work on the other 39 units was undertaken at Saint Ouen depot, following deliveries of new MF67 stock to line 9, which reduced the amount of work to be done at that depot on the old Classic stock. The work on the MA52 stock was also to improve its reliability, and to give it a new lease of life. It was completed by the autumn of 1976 and allowed the replacement of the 1926–36 Sprague stock on line 10.

On the modernised MA52 stock, the position of the first class accommodation was also altered, as on line 10 the units would not be required to uncouple, and the first class was thus moved to the standard position in the middle of the train. This was achieved by converting one motor car of half of the 40 units and ensuring that they were always formed in the middle of a train. The odd-numbered motor car of each odd-numbered unit was selected for first class accommodation and therefore each train comprises one odd and one even-numbered unit, until recently usually in adjacent numbered pairs (eg E001+E002). With semi-permanent train formations, the middle driving cabs became redundant, only equipment needed for shunting being retained (and locked away out of use when in service, so that the area could be used by passengers). As line 10 has a loop at its western end, trains do not always remain facing the same way round, and if it is necessary to substitute a unit for maintenance, it is sometimes possible to see a single unit working an empty 'turning' trip from Auteuil to Duroc and back. The traffic levels, and as a result, service intervals, on line 10 do not warrant the investment of Automatic Train Operation, and thus the MA52 stock operates in conventional driving mode. However, line 10 is now one-person-operated and the trains have additional safety features incorporated. The system is known as CMC (manual driving control) and at each driving position, a ring around the controller is provided, as well as a foot pedal. Either of these must be operated by the driver at intervals not exceeding 30 seconds and should this not be done, a warning bell will sound in the cab. If one or the other is not operated after a further 2½ seconds, the train will be halted by the application of the emergency brake, and an alarm will sound in the control room (PCC).

The MA52 stock, now over 35 years old, is approaching the end of its working life. It is to be replaced (indirectly) by new MF88 stock and the transfer of spare MF67 stock from lines 9 and 12. (It should be noted that, since 1975, line 10 has had a small number of MF67 trains, to supplement the MA52 stock, as the latter are insufficient in total to provide the complete service on line 10). The first withdrawals of MA52 stock occurred in July 1987 with units E019+E020 stored at Saint-Ouen depot. E015 and E016 were withdrawn and loaned to the manufacturer, Alsthom, for experimental purposes in December 1987, while E037 was withdrawn in March 1988 and E001 in April 1988. One car of E001 was taken by road from Villette in May 1988 to the RATP's Technical School.

For the enthusiast, the articulated stock is well worth a visit, with its quite musical qualities and Westinghouse air brakes. The RATP deserves every credit for experimenting with articulation at a time (in the early 1950s) when it was not as fashionable in urban transport as it is now.

The 'Pneu' Stock

The need for greater line capacity than could be obtained with conventional stock, and the great expense of lengthening stations to allow longer trains to be operated, caused a novel alternative to be considered by the RATP. Greater line capacity was to be obtained with the aid of the high acceleration and retardation given by the use of rubber tyres, and higher maximum speeds between closely spaced stations could be given by the same means. Extra comfort and lightweight vehicles would also be obtained.

Plans were thus formulated for experiments with rubber-tyred train operation. The 767m long 'shuttle' line between Porte des Lilas and Pré-Saint-Gervais was chosen, which had been closed to passengers since September 1939, and a special single car was built in 1951 by a consortium of manufacturers, with two 130hp Alsthom motors and Jeumont equipment. The motors were hung from the body, instead of being mounted on the bogies in the usual way, and drove the axles by cardan drive. A small pantograph, not normally visible, was fitted for shunting purposes. For the first time, rheostatic braking was fitted, backed up by electro-pneumatic brakes, with automatic deceleration and braking for normal service. The coach was classified '**MP51**' and carried the stock number of 151 at each end. It was delivered on 25 July 1951 and was made available for inspection by the press and the public on 12 and 14 November 1951. The coach underwent exhaustive tests and trials and entered service on 13 April 1952 carrying passengers between 13.30 and 19.30 on the shuttle line. The trials also included experiments with Automatic Train Operation. The car was withdrawn from service on 31 May 1956 and, being an experiment, the service was not replaced. The car was put into store in 1961 and in April 1981 was taken to the Paris Transport Museum at Saint Mandé where it was put on display to the public, representing a very important stage in the transition of Paris Métro rolling stock.

For rubber-tyred train operation, the track has to be specially converted. It consists of conventional steel rails, which are retained as 'safety' rails, flanked by longitudinal bearing strips for the rubber tyred wheels, at 1.98m gauge. These strips were of tropical hardwood (now replaced), of reinforced concrete, or of wide metal 'I' beams. Vertical guide bars, which are also the conductor rails, are arranged 2.44m apart on insulating supports.

The bogies have rubber-tyred carrying wheels with tyres 1m in diameter, inflated to $9kg/cm^2$ (motor) or $6.5kg/cm^2$ (trailers). Inside there are conventional steel wheels with deep flanges which drop onto the safety rail if a tyre becomes deflated. Braking is by oiled-wood blocks onto these wheels. Shoes rubbing on the safety rails give both negative return and track circuit operation for automatic signalling. Spring-loaded shoes press sideways onto the guide bars for current collection. Guide wheels on vertical axles fit between the guide bars – their tyres are 0.54m diameter, inflated to $9kg/cm^2$.

At points and crossings, the longitudinals are lowered to the level of the steel rails and the guide rails interrupted; the deep flanges of the steel wheels then guide the train. Severe speed limits are in force at these locations.

The prototype 'pneu' car, MP51, or 151, is now on display in the Saint Mandé Transport Museum, showing the special track arrangements necessary for the running of rubber-tyred trains. The rear track-level view of an MP55A motor car shows the horizontal guide wheel tyre, the guide rail and the (now extinct) wooden running surfaces for the main tyres. *Brian Patton*

From these experiments it was decided that the idea of rubber-tyred train operation on the Métro was sound and the whole of line 11 was chosen for conversion to 'pneu' operation. Although a relatively short line, 6.287km from Châtelet to Mairie des Lilas, it nevertheless had a wide variety of technical problems to offer, such as many curves and an almost continuous gradient at 1 in 25. The new stock for line 11 was formed into four-car sets formed of two driving motor cars (M), one non-driving motor car (N) and one composite trailer (AB), in the formation M – N – AB – M. Known as the **MP55** type, it was built in two separate batches, as follows:

Type		
MP55A	M3001-3020	Bodies and bogies by RNUR, equipment by CEM
MP55A	N4001-4010	
MP55A	AB5501-5510	
MP55B	M3021-3036	Bodies by Brissonneau et Lotz, bogies by Alsthom, equipment by Jeumont
MP55B	N4011-4018	
MP55B	AB5511-5517	

The main difference between this stock and its predecessors lies, of course, with its bogies, but the opportunity was taken to introduce some modifications in design of the bodywork to improve the general standard of comfort offered to the travelling public. Despite being of two different batches, however, all were operationally compatible.

The driving cars are 15m long, the non-driving cars and trailers 14.39m. To improve passenger flow, the width of the door openings was increased to 1.30m. The doors are operated pneumatically and can be opened by simply raising a latch as the train comes to a halt. When closing, the rate of travel slows down as the doors come together, in marked contrast to the Sprague stock, whose doors met with a hefty 'clump', and in their day no doubt accounted for many a crushed finger! Lighting and suspension were improved and, for the first time, sliding ventilators were fitted to the windows – on both sides of the car. Partly because of these, the noise level was reduced considerably. Internally, the cars were much like the articulated MA52 stock and they were painted in the same livery.

Each motor car has four 90hp axle-hung motors and JH-type cam-contactor controllers are fitted. Acceleration progresses under time control so that it is much the same whether the train is empty or full; the acceleration and deceleration rates of $1.3m/s^2$ (compared with 0.7 on the Sprague stock) and $1.45m/s^2$ (which can be increased to $2.5m/s^2$ in emergency), together with the excellent adhesion given by rubber tyres, gives these trains very good performance, even on the severe curves and gradients of line 11.

Work on converting the trackwork on line 11 commenced in 1954 and the first train of MP55 stock entered service on 11 November 1956. Other trains followed up to October 1957. From the numbering of the stock, 17 four-car trains can be formed, leaving two driving motor cars and one non-driving motor car spare. These in fact did not enter service until required much later (3036 in February 1958, 3021 in April 1958 and 4018 in April 1961) and thus it will be appreciated that formations are not constant. This has become more evident in later years when, from 1977, a programme of renovation began, to bring the MP55 cars up to the standard of the MP73 type (q.v. below). Work included increasing the fluorescent lighting and fitting outside door indicator lights. Ventilation was also improved by fitting directional vents. The renovation of the cars was done singly and coincided with repainting into royal blue and white livery. Thus, trains could be seen in service in both liveries and in modified or unmodified form. On the driving motor cars, the area surrounding the cab windows was painted black at first, presumably to give the impression of a one-piece screen that later MP stocks had. However, some have also been outshopped with white-painted cab window surrounds. Three cars have been out of use since 1979. One is used at the Sucy experimental centre as a Tracteur, the other two being stored.

The line 11 'pneu' conversion was considered very much still an experiment, but its success prompted the RATP to begin a programme of conversion of all its lines, starting with line 1, then line 4, the two busiest Métro lines. It took a considerable period of time, however, to convert the trackwork, and then another year or so to introduce the rolling stock – the complete line's trackwork had to be converted before even one 'pneu' train could operate. On line 1, track conversion took place from 1960 and new rolling stock was introduced between 31 May 1963 and December 1964. The conversion of line 4 followed and the stock was phased in from 3 October 1966 until August 1967. The rolling stock for both lines 1 and 4 was of one type – the **MP59** – but was delivered in three batches of four groups, the last of which was not delivered until 1972/73 to supplement existing trains on those two lines for increased services. All MP59 trains were built by CIMT with ANF bogies and Jeumont equipment and were formed into six-car trains, comprising two driving motor cars (M), two non-driving motor cars (N), one composite trailer (AB) and one first class trailer (A): M – N – AB – A – N – M.

The stock was numbered as follows:

Type		
MP59A	M3037-3128	
MP59A	N4019-4110	
MP59A	AB5518-5563	1963-64 for line 1
MP59A	A6001-6046	
MP59B	M3129-3158	
MP59B	N4111-4140	
MP59B	AB5564-5576	
MP59B	A6047-6059	
MP59C	M3159-3224	1966-67 for line 4
MP59C	N4141-4206	
MP59C	AB5577-5607	
MP59C	A6060-6090	
MP59D	M3225-3240	
MP59D	N4207-4222	
MP59D	AB5608-5616	1972-73 for lines 1 and 4
MP59D	A6091-6100	

The sharpest curve on the Métro used by passenger trains is at Bastille on line 1, the only open-air section on this line. A train of MP59 stock in new livery negotiates the curve arriving, while the train on the right is still in old livery.

R.J. Greenaway

Interior view of MP59 stock. The spaced fluorescent lighting is still as originally fitted to the MA52 and MP55 stocks.
R.J. Greenaway

Bastille station on line 1 in September 1987, with a train of MP59 stock in the old livery. The cream first class trailer A6033 is next to the former composite, numbered 5542; still prefixed 'AB', although the class numbers at the top of the doors have been amended to '2'.
Brian Hardy

The most noticeable difference between the earlier 'pneu' trains (the MP55) on line 11 and the later ones of lines 1 and 4 (MP59) is the adoption of a wide single-span windscreen on the driving cabs of the latter trains. On these, the traction motors are rated at 140hp as against 90hp of the MP55 cars. One of the additional trains built in 1973 (3235-4217-6096-5613-4218-3236) was equipped with thyristor 'chopper' control, operating in service on line 1 until 1979, then on line 4. It was sub-classified MP59DK and was converted to MP59D standard in 1985.

The six-car formations of MP59 stock in fact comprised about one car and one third of another with first class accommodation. In the early 1980s, the policy of first class accommodation on the Métro was changed, with the attitude towards making a reduction in its hours of operation. During 1981-83, all the composite cars on lines 1 and 4 were converted to second class, leaving one car out of six for first class passengers (compared to one out of five cars on most other lines), and from 1 March 1982, first class travel was restricted to between the hours of 09.00 and 17.00 daily. Previously it had applied from 08.00 and then throughout each day. Insofar as the MP59 'AB' cars were concerned, all that needed to be done was to alter the exterior '1' to '2' on the old-liveried cars, and to remove the yellow band from the newer-liveried cars. There is no difference, comfort-wise, in first class accommodation in the Métro nowadays – its only advantage is that one has less fellow travellers to share the car with! Car identification was changed from 'AB' to 'B'.

The original fleet of 607 MP59 cars (204 'M', 204 'N', 99 'AB' and 100 'A') has been reduced by three over the years, due to various mishaps. N4077 was withdrawn in 1977, N4069 in 1982 and M3073 in 1986.

A novel experiment took place on the MP59 stock in 1984. Trailer B5537 was fitted with television screens to show video films. The car operated on line 1 in a six-month trial, the front motor cars having 'Métro Video' flashes applied. A further trial with B5519 was intended, to the extent that seating was altered to test different position of the televisions, but this did not take place, and the original experiment has ended.

For reasons that will become apparent in the next rolling stock section (MF67), the RATP decided to abandon its plan to convert all Métro lines to 'pneu' operation, but a change of heart was made for line 6, which had much more open-air running (mostly on viaduct) than any other Métro line. This gave much noise and vibration with the old Sprague stock and this line was therefore an ideal candidate for rubber-tyred trains. Track conversion commenced in 1972 and new rolling stock of type **MP73** was built by CIMT with ANF bogies and Jeumont equipment. Surprisingly, for a rubber-tyred line, the rolling stock was introduced within the space of just one month – from July 1974 (the period of the year with the lowest peak traffic) with extra trains added in time for maximum winter service, which starts in October. Trains were formed into five cars: M – B – A – N – M. The bodywork design was based on the already successful MF67 stock (q.v. below), which by then had become the accepted design for new stock until the advent of the MF77 type. The cars were numbered as follows:

M3501 - 3602	N4501 - 4550	A6501 - 6550	B7001 - 7050

It is interesting to note that M3599/3600 served as prototypes for the Marseille Métro, and M3602 for the Lyon Métro. In addition, cars A6550 and N4550, both having experimental suspension, first entered service on line 1 with the MP59 stock and were painted in the old livery of that stock, while the rest of the MP73 type was in the royal blue and white livery. Both cars were repainted into standard colours when they went into service on line 6 in 1976.

Some trains of MP73 stock have been allocated to line 11 since January 1976, to supplement the MP55 trains and providing an increased service on that line. The MP73 sets on line 11 operate in four-car formation like the MP55s, with the relevant cars not required being stored. This is usually the 'B' car, with the 'A' car modified as a composite, but with the classification unchanged. A small number of MP73 cars also saw service on line 4 between 1975 and 1979.

The MP73 stock can thus mostly be found on line 6 and as this line contains several open-air sections, amounting to almost half the line's length, special features were incorporated in these trains. This includes weatherproof ventilation, windscreen wipers, grooved tyres, snowproof resistance grids and chassis parts in Corten rustproof alloy instead of steel. This was the first new stock for the Paris Métro to be delivered in the new royal blue and white livery, with a dark blue stripe at waist level, and first class indicated by a yellow band at roof line. Outside door indicator lights are fitted to these trains, after an experiment with a train of MP59 stock on line 4 (3231-4213-6001-(7004)-4214-3232), which incorporates an MP73 trailer. One car (A6504) was scrapped in 1977.

For the future, it is planned that a batch of **MP89** stock will be built for line 11, allowing the MP55 trains to be withdrawn and the MP73 to be transferred to line 1. The MP89 stock will be updated but standard 'pneu' trains. The MP59 trains on line 1 are to be renovated, as that line is to have an extension from Pont de Neuilly to La Défense opened in 1992 which will involve a short section of open-air running. For this, the line 1 MP59 stock will have to be fitted with window wipers, car heaters, sun blinds for drivers, while the door areas and electrical equipment will have to be waterproofed. This will allow these very reliable trains to continue in service for many more years, while in the mid-1990s, the MP59 stock on line 4 will be replaced.

It is interesting to note that the tyres on a 'pneu' train are changed at about every 450,000km, but visual checks on their condition are made at each maintenance session. There are, however, puncture (tyre pressure) detectors provided on the line; but that at Picpus on line 6 is computerised and is able to state the car position in the train, which axle, which wheel and whether to the left or the right side of the train. The detection of an incorrectly inflated tyre at this location will prevent the signal approaching the terminal station at Nation from clearing automatically, and thus the offending train has to be manually routed in for examination. It should be pointed out here that out of all four 'pneu' lines (1, 4, 6 and 11) the rate of flat tyres is, at worst, about one per month!

A five-car train of MP73 stock departs from La Motte Picquet on line 6, with the overall roof of the next station, Dupleix, visible in the background.
Brian Hardy

A 'pneu' bogie in Fontenay depot shows the wheel arrangements clearly, including the deep flanges of the steel (safety) wheels common to all 'pneu' trains.
Brian Hardy

The MF67 Stock

While the success of the rubber-tyred stock was undoubted, it took approximately three years to convert the trackwork and generally about another year to phase in the rolling stock, and at that rate it would have been impossible to have completed the modernisation of the Métro before the end of this century. Between 1951 and 1964 there were, too, considerable advances in the design of conventional rapid transit trains in other countries, and in 1964 the RATP began to study the development of modern rolling stock which would provide the same acceleration and braking characteristics, as well as the quiet and comfortable ride, as the 'pneu' trains. The result was the **MF67** stock, the first train of which went into service on line 3 on 21 December 1967.

Externally, the MF67 stock differed from the 'pneu' trains only in the restyled front end and driver's cab, and in its pull-down opening saloon windows instead of sliding vents. The trains are much quieter than the Classic stock; some have rubber sandwich wheels, a ring of rubber blocks being pressed between the steel tyres and the rims of the wheels. Rubber springing in the bogies and sound insulation of the bodies also contribute to the reduction of noise.

A standard formation of MF67 stock on line 9 at Michel-Ange-Auteuil, departing in the direction of Mairie de Montreuil, despite what is displayed on the rear destination blind.
R.J. Greenaway

The interior of M10207 of MF67C2 type at Porte des Lilas on line 3bis shows the vandal-resistant seating now being fitted. So far, stock on lines 3bis and 7bis have seats on this style as well as the MI84 and refurbished MS61 trains on RER line A.
R.J. Greenaway

The unpainted aluminium/stainless steel MF67W2 prototype, in service on line 9 in 1981 at Porte de Montreuil.

R.J. Greenaway

The MF67 cars have all axles driven and originally trains were formed of motor cars only, to give a performance approximate to that of the 'pneu' stock. Half the cars have monomotor bogies with a 194hp motor and half have two-motor bogies with two 99hp motors. Control is by servo-motor-operated cam-contactors with electronic control of the servo-motors to give smooth acceleration. Service braking is rheostatic down to low speeds with air taking over thereafter. In practice, the provision of all-motor-car trains proved to be over-generous and trailers were subsequently introduced in 1974. Normal train formation is now three motor cars and two trailers in a five-car set. Modifications introduced on successive batches of motor cars include regenerative braking, mechanical ventilation, disc brakes and air suspension. Internally, the MF67 stock has generous lighting by fluorescent tubes and comfortable leatherette seating. Some of the prototypes, however, have a different cosmetic finish. Loudspeakers allow the driver to address the passengers and the MF67E stock on line 2 has been modified so that there is two-way communication between the driver and passengers should an emergency handle be operated, a feature first adopted on the MF77 trains. Door indicator lights are fitted to the car exteriors, so that staff can easily identify faulty doors.

Whilst in general terms the MF67 type is grouped into six sub classes, (generally designated MF67A to MF67F) when analysed in depth there are in fact 15 different types, each having slight differences, generally in equipment, but sometimes in cosmetic finishes. For example, one train was delivered in unpainted aluminium/stainless steel.

Following the entry into service of the first (prototype) train (type 'W1') on line 3 in December 1967, production started of the 'A' series, entering service on line 3 from August 1968, formed into five-car all motor car trains: M – N – NA – N – M. The order also comprised the unpainted/stainless steel train (type 'W2') and six single cars of types 'B1' and 'B2'. The 'A' series comprised two types – the 'A1' with monomotor bogies and the 'A2' with bi-motor bogies. The last of this series went into service on line 3 in January 1970, making a total of 42 five-car trains, including the prototypes and the experimental cars.

The next line to receive MF67 stock was line 7 from June 1971. Prior to this, a new series of MF67 stock commenced delivery – the 'C1' – from early-1971, first entering service on line 3 from April. This allowed the release of the 'A2' type from line 3 to line 7 and from December 1971 a further new batch of type 'C2' entered service directly on line 7, the last to do so being in January 1974. This segregated the stocks so that the trains with monomotor bogies were all on line 3 and those with bi-motors were on line 7. All three types 'A', 'B' and 'C' and their variations were built by CIMT and Brissonneau et Lotz.

Included in the prototype cars and trains were two trailers, one of which was finished in unpainted aluminium/stainless steel. These two trailers entered service in late 1969 and early 1970 to evaluate the performance of trains that were not formed of all motor cars, being transferred to line 7 in November 1971.

The dilution of train sets with trailers was successful and it allowed the RATP to reduce both capital and operating costs. The next order for MF67 stock therefore comprised all trailers – both driving and non-driving – built jointly by Alsthom and SFB from mid-1974 to early 1976, the first examples entering service on line 3 in September 1974 (trailers) and on line 9 (driving trailers). These trailers (156 driving trailers coded 'S', 145 second class trailers coded 'B' and 62 first class trailers coded 'A') were known as MF67 type 'D'.

Non-driving motor car N11075 from line 10 in overhauled condition at Choisy depot in September 1987. This car, new in 1969, still awaits its first repaint, which will be done separately, at Fontenay. Rolling stock operating on wholly tunnel sections of line is repainted about every 17 years. *Brian Hardy*

Prototype MF67W2 trailer B14002 at Louise Michel on line 3 in February 1988. This shows clearly its stainless steel finish, although now painted into the new livery. *R.J. Greenaway*

A train of MF67E stock approaches Jaurès on the elevated section of line 2. In the right foreground can be seen a high-quality reflective OPO mirror, pioneered on the Brussels Métro. Above this in the background can be seen the restricted visibility bar/circle symbols.
Brian Hardy

A carefully prepared plan involving the reformation of the all-motor sets on lines 3 and 7 was implemented. On line 3, the two 'N' cars were removed and replaced by 'B' trailers, giving a formation of M – B – NA – B – M. On line 7, one 'N' and one 'NA' was removed and replaced by a new 'B' and 'A' respectively, giving a formation of M – B – A – N – M. The new driving trailers ('S') were formed with displaced 'N' and 'NA' cars, forming trains thus: S – N – NA – N – S. These went into service on lines 9 and 13, with a small allocation to line 10 to supplement the articulated stock then being transferred from line 13. To complete this plan, four non driving motors (N11131-11134) were converted to first class accommodation, becoming NA12129-12132 in 1974. It is interesting to note that the MF67D stock had to be delivered in the old pale blue livery (first class cars cream) to match the older cars of MF67 stock that they were being formed with, even though previous new stock (the MP73 for line 6) had been delivered in the new royal blue and white livery.

A further two batches of MF67 stock were yet to be built, but these were not generally to be mixed with the A-D type. The next batch was the MF67 type 'E' and these five car trains in the new livery from new were built by CIMT and entered service on line 8 from 14 July 1975, with some going to line 13. The delivery of this stock to line 8 allowed some of the grey Sprague stock to be transferred to line 2 (and later, lines 9 and 12), then seeing the end of two-motor Sprague stock on line 2 on 22 March 1976.

The final batch of MF67 stock was the type 'F' built by BL. These trains, also five cars in length, had interior fans fitted for improved ventilation and were instantly recognisable from the outside by having a smoother finish to the roof line. They first entered service on line 13 from October 1976, displacing the MF67E type on that line to join their sister cars on line 8.

Because of the open-air stabling of trains on line 5 at Bobigny, a programme commenced in mid-1987 of encasing the sliding door areas on MF67F stock, reducing the window opening area to a short single-glazed centre section. M10512 in modified condition leads a train into Quai de la Rapée, showing also the improved roof line of this (last) batch of MF67 stock, having mechanical ventilation fitted. *R.J. Greenaway*

Interior of MF67F stock on line 5, showing the fans situated along the car ceiling. *R.J. Greenaway*

   With the advent of the MF77 stock, which first went to line 13, the displaced MF67F trains were transferred to line 7, which allowed the diluted M – B – A – N – M formations of the A–D type to be transferred to lines 9 and 12. In fact both these lines operated formations of M – B – A – N – M and S – N – NA – N – S. Some of the latter driving trailer sets also went to line 5 from April 1978, and to line 2 from February 1979.
   Deliveries of the MF77 stock then went to lines 7 (from September 1979) and 8 (from July 1980), which released the MF67F from line 7 to go to line 5, and the MF67E from line 8 to line 2. The earlier A-D types on line 2 went to line 12, finishing off the Sprague stock on that line in December 1980, followed by line 2 in June 1981. Enough MF67F trains were available from line 7 to replace the Sprague stock on line 7bis from July 1980, which

operated in full-length five-car formations, while from mid-1981 a sufficient number of MF67E trains were available to replace the Sprague stock on line 3bis, but in three-car formations, the other two cars of the set being stored. To give a section of first class accommodation on these three-car sets, a small portion of the middle trailer was converted as such and were temporarily classified as 'Ba'. This arrangement on the two branch lines was short-lived and a more permanent stock situation was established. From February 1982, the five-car trains of MF67F stock on line 7bis were transferred back to line 7 (and subsequently to line 5), being replaced by four-car sets of MF67E from line 3bis, the first class trailer in the formation being brought back out of store. On line 3bis, three-car trains of MF67A-D type were transferred in from line 9, in the same formation of M-Ba-M.

Other rolling stock displacement has been the MF67F now on line 5, supplemented by four trains of the driving trailer formation (MF67D); the other driving trailer formations are the only type on line 12 and a smaller number are on lines 9 and 10. Line 9, however, has mostly trains composed M – N – A – B – M.

The MF67 stock can now therefore be found in service on eight Métro lines, in formations as follows:

	Type	Formation
Line 2	MF67E	M — B — A — N — M
Line 3	MF67A-D	M — B — NA — B — M*
Line 3bis	MF67A-D	M — Ba — M
Line 5	MF67A-D	S — N — NA — N — S
	MF67F	M — N — A — B — M
Line 7bis	MF67E	M — N — A — M
Line 9	MF67A-D	S — N — NA — N — S
	MF67A-D	M — N — A — B — M†
Line 10	MF67A-D	S — N — NA — N — S
Line 12	MF67A-D	S — N — NA — N — S

*2 trains are M – N – NA – N – M
†1 train is M – N – NA – N – M

MF67 STOCK SUMMARY

Stock Type	M	N	NA	A	B	S	Total
MF67 W1	2	2	1	–	1	–	6
MF67 W2	2	2	1	–	1	–	6
MF67 A1	36	40	20	–	–	–	96
MF67 A2	39	39	20	–	–	–	98
MF67 B1	4	–	–	–	–	–	4
MF67 B2	1	1	–	–	–	–	2
MF67 C1	44	40	26	–	–	–	110
MF67 C1A	2	2	1	–	–	–	5
MF67 C2	91	91	46	–	–	–	228
MF67 C2A	2	2	1	–	–	–	5
MF67 CS	2	2	1	–	–	–	5
MF67 CX	–	7	9	–	–	–	16
MF67 D	–	–	–	62	145	156	363
MF67 E	114	56	–	56	56	–	282
MF67 F	104	51	–	51	51	–	257
Total:	443	335	126	169	254	156	1483

The numbers and 15 variations of the MF67 Stock can be summarised as follows:

Type	Numbers	New	Details
MF67W1	M10001-10002 N11001-11002 NA12001 B14001	1967 1970	Built by CIMT, Düwag monomotor bogies, CEM and Siemens equipment. B14001 has MF77 type interior.
MF67W2	M10003-10004 N11003-11004 NA12002 B14002	1968 1969	Built by Brissonneau et Lotz, ANF bimotor bogies, Alsthom equipment. Stainless steel/ unpainted body by Carel-Fouché, saving 700kg weight per car, but more expensive to produce and therefore not pursued. B14002 now repainted into the new blue livery.
MF67A1	M10011-10019 M10021-10023 M10026-10027 M10029-10050 N11011-11050 NA12011-12030	1968	Built by CIMT, Düwag monomotor bogies, CEM equipment. Rheostatic/disc braking.
MF67A2	M10051-10053 M10055-10090 N11051-11053 N11055-11090 NA12031-12050	1969	Built by Brissonneau et Lotz, ANF bimotor bogies, Alsthom equipment. Conventional brake blocks, rheostatic braking.
MF67B1	M10020 M10024-10025 M10028	1969	Built by Brissonneau et Lotz, CEM equipment. Experimental monomotor bogies by MTE (10020), Alsthom (10024), ANF (10025) and CAFL (10028).
MF67B2	M10054 N11054	1969	Built by Brissonneau et Lotz, Alsthom equipment, ANF bimotor bogies with air suspension.
MF67C1	M10091-10134 N11091-11130 NA12051-12072 NA12129-12132	1971	CIMT bodies and monomotor bogies, CEM equipment. Rheostatic/disc braking.
MF67C1A	M10007-10008 N11007-11008 NA12004	1973	CIMT aluminium bodies, Düwag monomotor bogies; CEM/Jeumont equipment, pneumatic suspension, interior fans for mechanical ventilation.
MF67C2	M10135-10224 M10227 N11135-11224 N11227 NA12073-12118	1971	Built by Brissonneau et Lotz, ANF bimotor bogies, Alsthom equipment, conventional brake blocks, rheostatic braking.
MF67C2A	M10005-10006 N11005-11006 NA12003	1974	Built by Brissonneau et Lotz, ANF bimotor bogies, Alsthom equipment, pneumatic suspension and mechanical ventilation.
MF67CS	M10225-10226 N11225-11226 NA12119	1975	Built by Brissonneau et Lotz, MTE bogies with pneumatic suspension, Alsthom equipment, regenerative normal service braking and electro magnetic braking.

MF67CX	N11228-11234 NA12120-12128	1974	As type C2, but N11228 and 11234 fitted with plug doors, as similarly adopted on MF77 stock trains.
MF67D	S9011-9126 A13011-13052 B14011-14114	1974	Built by Alsthom. Standard block braking.
MF67D	S9127-9166 A13053-13072 B14115-14155	1974	Built by Alsthom. Standard block braking.
MF67E	M10301-10414 N11301-11356 A13301-13356 B14301-14356	1975	Built by CIMT, ANF bimotor bogies, Alsthom equipment, regenerative braking. First of MF67 type to be delivered in new royal blue/white livery. Bogies on N11332 and M10370 by Creusot Loire. B14311 with concealed lighting, fans and MI79 type grab stands/perches.
MF67F	M10501-10604 N11501-11551 A13501-13551 B14501-14551	1976	Built by Brissonneau et Lotz, ANF mono-motor bogies with pneumatic suspension, TCO equipment, disc/regenerative braking. Interior fans for mechanical ventilation, giving a smoother finish to the exterior roof line.

One of the driving trailer sets of MF67 stock on line 5 departing from Gare d'Austerlitz in 1981, on which line there are now only four in service. The rear car, S9030, went to line 9 in 1983 and to line 10 in 1986. *R.J. Greenaway*

The MF77 Stock

The extension of the Métro into the suburbs of Paris and the greater distance between stations on these extensions (800 to 1,000m as against about 500m in the City area) highlighted some of the weak points of existing designs and in 1972 the RATP instituted studies for the design of rolling stock which would be faster and more comfortable than existing trains, and more suited to suburban work. Experiments with various features, such as plug doors, internal decor etc, were made on various cars of MF67 stock and research was undertaken by industrial designers, acting in collaboration with both engineers and marketing specialists, and backed by surveys made among the travelling public to find out what they wanted in the new trains. A mock-up coach was built and exhibited at the 75th anniversary of the Métro at Porte Maillot station in 1975 which was in green and brown livery. The result of all this was the **MF77** stock, the first train of which entered service on line 13 in September 1978. The trains are formed into five-car sets (M – B – NA – B – M) and can now be found operating the complete services on lines 7, 8 and 13.

When the new trains appeared they showed an advance in design not only over existing Métro stock, but also over trains running on rapid transit systems elsewhere. The sides of the cars are not straight, unlike all previous Métro stock, but curve outwards to give the maximum width at waist level consistent with the constraints of the loading gauge. This, together with the use of plug-type doors instead of ones sliding back into recesses, has

The mock-up of the MF77 stock on display at Porte Maillot in 1975, during the Metro's 75th anniversary.
R.J. Greenaway

The finished MF77 product in service on line 8 at République. A total of 197 five-car trains of this type were built between 1977 and 1986, now providing the complete services on lines 7, 8 and 13. The doors open externally, as seen here in this February 1988 view.
R.J. Greenaway

Interior view of MF77 stock motor car M30109 showing the individual seat pairs and concealed fluorescent lighting.
R.J. Greenaway

given a total increase in width of 140mm at the shoulder level of seated passengers. The unusual (for Paris Métro) shape of the cars is set off by a striking livery of off-white, relieved only by dark blue panels round the windscreens of the driving motor cars. First class accommodation is indicated by a yellow band at cantrail level. The cars are also slightly longer (15.110m on motor cars and 15.120m on trailers and non-driving motor cars) and in fact at some of the shorter stations, the head of the train is actually in the tunnel during stops. The new cars have only three pairs of doors per side as against four in previous stocks, but the door openings are much wider, at 1.575m instead of 1.30m, thus allowing a rapid flow of passengers. Push-button door control, comprising a button concealed in a shell grip, allows passengers to open individual pairs of doors once the train has stopped at a station, rather than by lifting a latch as hitherto.

Internally, the MF77 trains are distinguished by a harmony of muted tones, in contrast to the striking colour schemes favoured for other contemporary stock elsewhere. The seat colour is dark blue, walls are light blue and the doors, grab rails etc., are finished in stainless steel. The floors are covered with rubber matting. The space between the seats has been increased from 48cm to 54cm, to give improved comfort to seated passengers. All the materials used in the interior furnishings are, or have been treated to be, fire resistant. Lighting is by fluorescent tubes but, to reduce glare, is placed behind grilles which run the length of the ceiling and incorporate fans for ventilation. Seating is provided by individual pairs of seats instead of pairs of benches, and those at the non-driving ends of the cars are arranged in groups of three to face each other, giving the effect of a small saloon. The former tip-up perches have been replaced by proper folding seats, just as comfortable as the main seating. Heating and ventilation is thermostatically controlled. In addition to the windows in the communicating doors between the cars, windows are also provided either side of these at the trailing ends. This helps to create an atmosphere of spaciousness and a feeling of security which, with the high standard of design, gives a pleasant and relaxing effect overall.

The car body is made of light alloy sections, giving a saving of two tonnes in weight over a comparable train of steel construction. The driving cabs of the trains were designed after considerable ergonomic study and are laid out in such a way as to afford maximum convenience and comfort to the drivers. As on stock since the MP55 type, a speedometer and tachograph are fitted and three groups of colour light signals convey information about the running of the train and the functioning or non-functioning, of the equipment. As on all modern stock, a high-frequency telephone link keeps the drivers in touch with the PCC, but an innovation on the MF77 stock is a two-way link bewteen the driver and passengers, which comes into action when the emergency alarm signal has been actuated, in addition to the normal public address equipment.

The MF77 trains were built by SFB and Alsthom, the main order comprising 187 five-car trains, between 1978 and 1982. A further order for ten trains was built by Alsthom in 1986, to provide the stock required for the extensions to line 7. The MF77 trains are fitted with MTE-type bogies of the type already in use on the MF67F trains. Equipment is provided by TCO. There are six motor bogies on each five-car train and each motor bogie has a 266kW motor installed lengthwise between the two axles, in the centre of the bogie frame. On motor cars there is regenerative braking, plus air brakes, while on trailers braking is by compressed air alone.

Traction and braking control is performed by thyristor-equipped current choppers. The choppers do away with rheostats, which had hitherto been used to start the motors. They ensure far greater operating versatility and also cut down consumption while enabling power to be recovered on braking furnished by the motors operating as generators, which is fed back to the power line. Thus, the energy saving on a line equipped with modern cars can reach 40% compared with conventional trains with rheostatic starting and devoid of regenerative braking. In this way, the energy which was unnecessarily dissipated as heat is now recovered, the temperature in the Métro is reduced and comfort is enhanced.

The first train of MF77 stock was made available to the press at the SFB factory in Valenciennes on 25 October 1977, and in December it was exhibited to the public at Châtelet-les-Halles station on the RER. The first train to be delivered to Vaugirard depot arrived on 23 June 1978, and underwent exhaustive testing. Deliveries allowed the first train to enter service on line 13 in September 1978 and the following year line 7 was the next recipient of the MF77 stock, although it was not until 1985 that the last of the MF67F type was transferred away from line 7 to line 5. Line 13 had all MF77 trains by the end of 1979. In 1980 line 8 began to receive MF77 stock, replacing the MF67E type.

The last train of the main order of MF77 stock entered service on 2 February 1983 and subsequently allowed, through cascades of other stock, the last of the Sprague stock to be withdrawn.

The additional ten trains of MF77 stock for the line 7 extensions were delivered between September 1985 and July 1986, all entering service (on line 13, with other MF77 trains transferred to line 7) during 1986.

Built by SFB:

M30001-30074	B32001-32074	NA31001-31037
M30119-30158	B32119-32158	NA31060-31079
M30219-30252	B32219-32252	NA31110-31126
M30295-30328	B32295-32328	NA31148-31164
M30365-30370	B32365-32370	NA31183-31185

Built by Alsthom:

M30075-30118	B32075-32118	NA31038-31059
M30159-30218	B32159-32218	NA31080-31109
M30253-30294	B32253-32294	NA31127-31147
M30329-30364	B32329-32364	NA31165-31182
M30371-30374	B32371-32374	NA31186-31187
M30375-30394*	B32375-32394*	NA31188-31197*

Note *Includes 20 'M', 20 'B' and 10 'NA' of 1985-86 batch
    M30154 and B32154 scrapped April 1984.

Middle first class non-driving motor car NA31030 at Choisy depot shows the windows fitted to the ends of the saloons on MF77 stock. *Brian Hardy*

Three different types of current collector shoes on MF77 stock, but each bogie having air suspension. Note that on M30155 electro-magnetic track brakes are fitted; only two trains are now so equipped, although ten trains at one time used to have this feature. *R.J. Greenaway*

The Future

The RATP have been actively engaged in planning for future Métro rolling stock since 1980, of the steel-wheel-on-steel-rail type. The results of studies and tests is the 'BOA', a fully articulated train using single axles instead of bogies, thus providing the train with steered axles without the extra weight and complication of a steerable bogie. The first prototype train was designed and built by the RATP themselves in Vaugirard depot and consisted of three 10m articulated cars with monomotor axles. Apart from the articulation and the inter-connection between axles, all parts used were already on other stocks, being well-tried and tested. For instance, the underfloor equipment is as used on MP73 stock, and the car bodies are most definitely MF77.

Tests commenced in February 1985, the new innovation being a great success. With the reduction in the weight of the train, it consumes less current and stress on curves is much reduced. It was also tested on the very sharp non-passenger loop at Porte Dauphine on line 2 without problems. Early in 1986 the system was adapted to have steerable axles at the front of the train instead of bogies, whereby the leading axle 'reads' the curvature of the track and then guides the second axle. The leading axle is non-load-bearing and has smaller wheels than on all other axles. These tests also included further adaptation for use on 'pneu' line 1, all being very satisfactory.

Following on from these tests, the next stage was to develop a train which would ultimately carry passengers and the original 'BOA' was returned to Vaugirard workshops to enable a four-bodied train to be constructed, each section 10m long. This will enable three different types of body articulation to be tested, one each by Faivley, ANF and Alsthom. Although the axle weight for the four-section 'BOA' will be about 15 tonnes per axle as against 11 tonnes per axle on MF77 stock, the use of axles instead of bogies results in a 20% weight saving, which in turn creates considerable economies in running costs.

Early days of testing with the 'BOA' prototype on 7 March 1985, posing at Pasteur on line 12, when it was a three-section train and before steerable axles had replaced bogies on the outer ends.   *RATP*

Tests with this train started in December 1987 and it is anticipated that passengers will be carried from the autumn of 1988 on line 7bis. This type of train formation allows continuous inter-car circulation by passengers.

Also under investigation is the use of asynchronous motors on this train, following trials on MF77 driving motor car M30125 and MF67 cars M10024 and M10025. Another development under consideration is fully automatic control of trains, with no-person-operation, which will require constant data transmission and multiplexing. Platform-edge doors will have to be fitted at stations and neither these nor the train doors will open unless they are both in alignment.

The 'BOA' train is thus the prototype for the future **MF88** stock for line 7bis, which will ultimately allow, through consequential inter-line stock transfers, the withdrawal of the oldest Métro trains now in service – the articulated MA52 type on line 10. The production MF88 trains are likely to be 15m three-section versions of the 'BOA' prototype, of which ten trains in total will be required. The prototype is numbered M30411-N11552-N11553-M30412.

Looking down on the articulated section of the 'BOA' in Vaugirard depot, showing the inter-car connections, different door sections, and the axle-wheels themselves. *RATP*

Current collector shoes as found on conventional Métro stock (left) and for operating on 'pneu' lines (right), as fitted to an MF67 train for stock transfer purposes. *R.J. Greenaway*

TRAIN FORMATIONS

Formations are normally listed in the numerical order of the centre (first class) trailer. Formations may, from time to time, be changed.

LINE 1 — 48 x 6-car trains type MP59

3037	4031	6002	5563	4096	3076	3117	4037	6026	5528	4092	3056
3077	4085	6003	5547	4098	3106	3067	4029	6027	5550	4086	3114
3131	4089	6004	5543	4052	3078	3115	4079	6028	5558	4038	3118
3111	4071	6005	5537	4046	3042	3113	4025	6029	5533	4090	3060
3093	4074	6006	5535	4056	3064	3097	4099	6030	5552	4064	3112
3081	4083	6007	5518	4020	3054	3103	4081	6031	5562	4024	3084
3071	4061	6008	5546	4102	3068	3065	4065	6032	5540	4088	3050
3127	4091	6009	5522	4082	3086	3121	4111	6033	5542	4110	3124
3063	4047	6010	5549	4054	3044	3049	4055	6034	5534	4022	3090
3101	4039	6011	5524	4036	3104	3055	4097	6035	5529	4080	3126
3039	4053	6012	5519	4060	3092	3133	4035	6036	5527	4042	3062
3105	4101	6013	5525	4108	3046	3061	4021	6037	5554	4030	3088
3137	4059	6014	5559	4068	3110	3083	4115	6038	5541	4044	3048
3069	4107	6015	5560	4048	3082	3087	4087	6039	5553	4084	3058
3089	4027	6016	5548	4076	3130	3129	4109	6040	5551	4116	3074
3107	4033	6017	5556	4050	3040	3051	4063	6041	5544	4106	3080
3099	4019	6018	5523	4040	3108	3057	4093	6042	5539	4114	3120
3053	4023	6019	5555	4066	3122	3091	4075	6043	5557	4070	3038
3109	4049	6020	5532	4094	3070	3059	4113	6044	5520	4078	3102
3119	4067	6021	5538	4028	3128	3043	4041	6045	5526	4112	3100
3045	4045	6022	5530	4100	3098	3213	4103	6046	5564	4120	3134
3047	4095	6023	5536	4062	3132	3123	4057	6047	5545	4032	3072
3079	4051	6024	5521	4026	3066	3075	4105	6094	5611	4058	3116
3085	4073	6025	5531	4072	3094	3095	4043	6100	5561	4104	3052

Spare Car:
3125
Line total: 289 cars.

LINE 2 — 46 x 5-car trains type MF67E

10301	14301	13301	11301	10302	10357	14329	13329	11329	10358
10303	14302	13302	11302	10304	10359	14330	13330	11330	10360
10333	14303	13303	11303	10306	10363	14332	13332	‡11332	10364
10307	14304	13304	11304	10308	10365	14333	13333	11333	10366
10309	14305	13305	11305	10350	10367	14334	13334	11334	10368
10311	14306	13306	11306	10312	10369	14335	13335	11335	‡10370
10315	14308	13308	11347	10316	10371	14336	13336	11336	10372
10305	14309	13309	11309	10400	10373	14337	13337	11337	10374
10319	14310	13310	11310	10320	10375	14338	13338	11354	10376
10321	†14311	13311	11311	10322	10377	14339	13339	11339	10413
10323	14312	13312	11312	10324	10379	14340	13340	11340	10380
10325	14313	13313	11313	10382	10381	14341	13341	11341	10326
10342	14322	13314	11314	10328	10383	14342	13342	11351	10384
10329	14315	13315	11315	10330	10385	14343	13343	11343	10386
10331	14316	13316	11316	10332	10387	14344	13344	11344	10388
10414	14317	13317	11317	10378	10390	14345	13345	11338	10397
10335	14318	13318	11318	10336	10391	14346	13346	11346	10392
10337	14319	13319	11319	10355	10393	14347	13347	11308	10394
10339	14320	13320	11320	10340	10327	14348	13348	11348	10396
10341	14321	13321	11321	10318	10317	14349	13349	11349	10398
10349	14323	13325	11325	10408	10399	14350	13350	11350	10395
10351	14324	13326	11326	10352	10401	14351	13351	11345	10402
10353	14327	13327	11327	10354	10407	14354	13354	11342	10389

Spare Car:
10310 (Experiments at Championnet)
‡Experimental bogies by Creusot Loire.
†Concealed lighting, fans and MI79-type grab stands.
Line total: 231 cars

LINE 3 — 44 x 5-car trains type MF67A-D

10117	14083	12001	14082	10118	10219	11210	12043	11214	10220
10007	11007	12004	11008	10008	10091	14017	12051	14044	10092
10011	14111	12011	14108	10012	10093	14135	12052	14136	10094
10013	14115	12012	14120	10014	10095	14035	12053	14032	10096
10015	14107	12013	14103	10016	10097	14139	12054	14140	10098
10017	14105	12014	14106	10018	10099	14031	12055	14060	10100
10019	14117	12015	14118	10020	10101	14143	12056	14144	10102
10021	14013	12016	14014	10022	10103	14061	12057	14036	10104
10023	14011	12017	14012	10002	10105	14063	12058	14062	10106
10001	14113	12018	14112	10026	10107	14151	12059	14152	10108
10027	14045	12019	14030	10028	10109	14071	12060	14070	10110
10029	14109	12020	14110	10030	10111	14155	12061	14154	10112
10031	14047	12021	14034	10032	10113	14075	12062	14074	10114
10033	14059	12022	14054	10034	10115	14079	12063	14078	10116
10035	14021	12023	14048	10036	10119	14087	12065	14086	10120
10037	14049	12024	14020	10038	10121	14089	12066	14088	10122
10039	14051	12025	14114	10040	10123	14097	12067	14096	10124
10041	14037	12026	14050	10042	10125	14101	12068	14102	10126
10043	14026	12027	†14002	10044	10127	14099	12069	14098	10128
10045	14127	12028	14128	10046	10129	14104	12070	14100	10130
10047	14039	12029	14038	10048	10131	14145	12071	14146	10132
10049	14043	12030	14042	10050	10133	14015	12072	14016	10134

Spare Cars:
10024, 10025, 11127, 12064, 14355
†Ex-unpainted stainless steel car now in new livery.
Line total: 225 cars

LINE 3bis — 6 x 3-car trains type MF67A-D

10215	14023	10216	10213	14092	10214
10211	14046	10212	10217	14093	10218
10209	14091	10210	10207	14142	10208

Line total: 18 cars

LINE 4 — 52 x 6-car trains type MP59

†3231	4213	6001	‡7004	4214	3232	3179	4161	6073	5590	4162	3180
3207	4189	6048	5565	4190	3208	3215	4197	6074	5591	4198	3216
3191	4173	6049	5566	4174	3192	3219	4201	6075	5592	4202	3220
3193	4175	6050	5567	4176	3194	3138	4195	6076	5593	4196	3214
3221	4203	6051	5568	4204	3222	3209	4191	6077	5594	4192	3210
3197	4179	6052	5569	4180	3198	3173	4155	6078	5595	4156	3174
3157	4159	6053	5570	4140	3158	3217	4199	6079	5596	4200	3218
3177	4159	6054	5571	4160	3178	3163	4145	6080	5597	4146	3164
3195	4177	6055	5572	4178	3196	3199	4181	6081	5598	4182	3200
3165	4147	6056	5573	4148	3166	3203	4185	6082	5599	4186	3204
3161	4143	6057	5574	4144	3162	3143	4125	6083	5600	4126	3144
3205	4187	6058	5575	4188	3206	3187	4169	6084	5601	4170	3188
3201	4183	6059	5576	4184	3202	3151	4133	6085	5602	4134	3152
3171	4153	6060	5577	4154	3172	3211	4193	6086	5603	4194	3212
3147	4129	6061	5578	4130	3148	3141	4123	6087	5604	4124	3142
3145	4127	6062	5579	4128	3146	3169	4151	6088	5605	4152	3170
3185	4167	6063	5580	4168	3186	3149	4131	6089	5606	4132	3150
3189	4171	6064	5581	4172	3190	3183	4165	6090	5607	4166	3184
3167	4149	6065	5582	4150	3168	3233	4207	6091	5608	4208	3234
3223	4205	6066	5583	4206	3224	3227	4209	6092	5609	4210	3228
3139	4121	6067	5584	4122	3140	3229	4211	6093	5610	4212	3230
3181	4163	6068	5585	4164	3182	3225	4215	6095	5612	4216	3226
3135	4117	6069	5586	4118	3136	3235	4217	6096	5613	4218	3236
3159	4141	6070	5587	4142	3160	3237	4219	6097	5614	4220	3238
3175	4157	6071	5588	4158	3176	3239	4221	6098	5615	4222	3240
3153	4135	6072	5589	4136	3154	3155	4137	6099	5616	4138	3156

Spare Car:
4119
†Whole train with outside door indicator lights.
‡MP73 stock trailer car.
Line total: 313 cars

LINE 5 — 4 x 5-car trains type MF67A-D
51 x 5-car trains type MF67F

9164	11163	12048	11171	9154	10549	14525	13525	11525	10550
9157	11057	12074	11055	9155	10551	14526	13526	11526	10552
9123	11203	12086	11230	9056	10553	11527	13527	14527	10554
9042	11169	12111	11179	9136	10555	14528	13528	11528	10556
10501	11501	13501	14501	10502	10557	14529	13529	11529	10558
10503	14502	13502	11502	10504	10559	11530	13530	14530	10560
10505	14503	13503	11503	10506	10561	14531	13531	11531	10562
10507	11504	13504	14504	10508	10563	11532	13532	14532	10564
10509	11505	13505	14505	10510	10565	14533	13533	11533	10566
10511	14506	13506	11506	10512	10567	14534	13534	11534	10568
10513	14507	13507	11507	10514	10569	11535	13535	14535	10570
10515	14508	13508	11508	10516	10571	14536	13536	11536	10572
10517	14509	13509	11509	10518	10573	14537	13537	11537	10574
10519	14510	13510	11510	10520	10575	11538	13538	14538	10576
10521	11511	13511	14511	10522	10577	14539	13539	11539	10578
10523	14512	13512	11512	10524	10579	14540	13540	11540	10580
10525	14513	13513	11513	10526	10581	11541	13541	14541	10582
10527	11514	13514	14514	10528	10583	11542	13542	14542	10584
10603	11515	13515	14515	10529	10585	11543	13543	14543	10586
10531	11516	13516	14516	10532	10587	14544	13544	11544	10588
10533	11517	13517	14517	10534	10589	11545	13545	14545	10590
10535	14518	13518	11518	10536	10591	11546	13546	14546	10592
10537	14519	13519	11519	10538	10593	11547	13547	14547	10594
10539	14520	13520	11520	10540	10595	11548	13548	11548	10596
10541	11521	13521	14521	10542	10597	14549	13549	11549	10598
10543	11522	13522	14522	10544	10599	14550	13550	11550	10600
10545	14523	13523	11523	10546	10604	14551	13551	11551	10602
10547	14524	13524	11524	10548					

Spare Cars:
10530, 10601
Note that the MF67F stock is having saloon window modifications carried out.
Line total: 277 cars

LINE 6 — 43 x 5-car trains type MP73

3501	7001	6501	4501	3502	3551	7026	6526	4526	3552
3505	7003	6503	4503	3506	3553	7027	6527	4527	3554
3597	7005	6505	4549	‡3602	3555	7028	6528	4528	3556
3595	7007	6507	4548	3596	3557	7029	6529	4529	3558
3515	7008	6508	4508	3516	3559	7030	6530	4530	3560
3517	7009	6509	4509	3518	3561	7031	6531	4531	3562
3519	7010	6510	4510	3520	3563	7032	6532	4532	3564
3521	7011	6511	4511	3598	3565	7033	6533	4533	3566
3523	7012	6512	4512	3524	3567	7034	6534	4534	3568
3525	7013	6513	4513	3526	3569	7035	6535	4535	3570
3527	7014	6514	4514	3528	3571	7036	6536	4536	3572
3529	7015	6515	4515	3530	3573	7037	6537	4537	3574
3531	7016	6516	4516	3532	3575	7038	6538	4538	3576
3533	7017	6517	4517	3534	3577	7039	6539	4539	3578
3535	7018	6518	4518	3536	3579	7040	6540	4540	3580
3537	7019	6519	4519	3538	3581	7041	6541	4541	3582
3539	7020	6520	4520	3540	3583	7042	6542	4542	3584
3541	7021	6521	4521	3542	3585	7043	6543	4543	3586
3543	7022	6522	4522	3544	3587	7044	6544	4544	3588
3545	7023	6523	4523	3546	3589	7045	6545	4545	3590
3547	7024	6524	4524	3548	3593	7048	6547	4547	3594
3549	7025	6525	4525	3550					

Spare Cars:
3522, 3601
‡Prototype bogies for Lyon Métro.
Line total: 217 cars

LINE 7 bis — 9 x 4-car trains type MF67E

10313	11307	13307	10314	10403	11352	13352	10404
10343	11322	13322	10344	10405	11353	13353	10406
10345	11323	13323	10346	10409	11355	13355	10410
10347	11324	13324	10348	10411	11356	13356	10412
10334	11328	13328	10356				

Line total: 36 cars

LINE 7 — 73 x 5-car trains type MF77

30025	32025	31013	32026	30026	30181	32181	31091	32182	30182
30027	32027	31014	32028	30028	30183	32183	31092	32184	30184
30045	32045	31023	32046	30046	30187	32187	31094	32188	30188
30047	32047	31024	32048	30048	30189	32189	31095	32190	30190
30049	32049	31025	32050	30050	30191	32191	31096	32192	30192
30051	32051	31026	32052	30052	30229	32229	31115	32230	30230
30053	32053	31027	32054	30054	30293	32293	31147	32294	30294
30057	32057	31029	32056	30056	30317	32317	31159	32318	30318
30059	32059	31030	32060	30060	30319	32319	31160	32320	30320
30061	32061	31031	32062	30062	30321	32321	31161	32322	30322
30063	32063	31032	32064	30064	30323	32323	31162	32324	30324
30065	32065	31033	32066	30066	30325	32325	31163	32326	30326
30067	32067	31034	32068	30068	30327	32327	31164	32328	30328
30069	32069	31035	32070	30070	30329	32329	31165	32330	30330
30071	32071	31036	32072	30072	30331	32331	31166	32332	30332
30073	32073	31037	32074	30074	30333	32153	31167	32334	30334
30075	32075	31038	32076	30076	30335	32335	31168	32336	30336
30077	32077	31039	32078	30078	30337	32337	31169	32338	30338
30079	32079	31040	32080	30080	30339	32339	31170	32340	30340
30081	32081	31041	32082	30082	30341	32341	31171	32342	30342
30101	32101	31051	32102	30102	30343	32343	31172	32344	30344
30103	32103	31052	32104	30104	30345	32345	31173	32346	30346
30105	32105	31053	32106	30106	30347	32347	31174	32348	30348
30111	32111	31056	32112	30112	30349	32349	31175	32350	30350
30115	32115	31058	32116	30116	30351	32351	31176	32352	30352
30119	32119	31060	32120	30120	30353	32353	31177	32354	30354
30121	32121	31061	32122	30122	30355	32355	31178	32356	30356
30123	32123	31062	32124	30124	30357	32357	31179	32358	30358
30159	32159	31080	32160	30160	30359	32359	31180	32360	30360
30161	32161	31081	32162	30162	30361	32361	31181	32362	30362
30163	32163	31082	32164	30164	30363	32363	31182	32364	30364
30165	32165	31083	32166	30166	30365	32365	31183	32366	30366
30167	32167	31084	32168	30168	30367	32367	31184	32368	30368
30169	32169	31085	32170	30170	30369	32369	31185	32370	30370
30171	32171	31086	32172	30172	30371	32371	31186	32372	30372
30177	32177	31089	32178	30178	30373	32373	31187	32374	30374
30179	32179	31090	32180	30180					

Spare Car:
32333
Line total: 366 cars

LINE 8 — 60 x 5-car trains type MF77

30029	32029	31015	32030	30030	30233	32233	31117	32234	30234
30031	32031	31016	32032	30032	30235	32235	31118	32236	30236
30033	32033	31017	32034	30034	30237	32237	31119	32238	30238
30035	32035	31018	32036	30036	30239	32239	31120	32240	30240
30039	32039	31020	32040	30040	30241	32241	31121	32242	30242
30083	32083	31042	32084	30084	30243	32243	31122	32244	30244
30085	32085	31043	32086	30086	30245	32245	31123	32246	30246
30087	32087	31044	32088	30088	30247	32247	31124	32248	30248
30113	32113	31057	32114	30114	30249	32249	31125	32250	30250
30173	32173	31087	32174	30174	30251	32251	31126	32252	30252
30175	32175	31088	32176	30176	30253	32253	31127	32254	30254
30185	32185	31093	32186	30186	30255	32255	31128	32256	30256
30193	32193	31097	32194	30194	30257	32257	31129	32258	30258
30195	32195	31098	32196	30196	30259	32259	31130	32260	30260
30197	32197	31099	32198	30198	30261	32261	31131	32262	30262
30199	32199	31100	32200	30200	30263	32263	31132	32264	30264
30201	32201	31101	32202	30202	30265	32265	31133	32266	30266
30203	32203	31102	32204	30204	30267	32267	31134	32268	30268
30205	32205	31103	32206	30206	30269	32269	31135	32270	30270
30207	32207	31104	32208	30208	30271	32271	31136	32272	30272
30209	32209	31105	32210	30210	30273	32273	31137	32274	30274
30211	32211	31106	32212	30212	30275	32275	31138	32276	30276
30213	32213	31107	32214	30214	30277	32277	31139	32278	30278
30215	32215	31108	32216	30216	30279	32279	31140	32280	30280
30217	32217	31109	32218	30218	30281	32281	31141	32282	30282
30219	32219	31110	32220	30220	30283	32283	31142	32284	30284
30223	32223	31112	32224	30224	30285	32285	31143	32286	30286
30225	32225	31113	32226	30226	30287	32287	31144	32288	30288
30227	32227	31114	32228	30228	30289	32289	31145	32290	30290
30231	32231	31116	32232	30232	30291	32291	31146	32292	30292

Line total: 300 cars

LINE 9 — 70 x 5-car trains type MF67A-D

10005	11005	12003	11006	10006	10089	14125	13030	11090	10090
9113	11143	12033	11067	9068	10135	14126	13031	11136	10136
9149	11153	12037	11174	9150	10137	14129	13032	11138	10138
9103	11079	12040	11145	9076	10139	14058	13033	11140	10140
9114	11088	12041	11082	9124	10141	14131	13034	11142	10142
9073	11173	12079	11147	9101	10143	14132	13035	11144	10144
9102	11177	12084	11181	9141	10187	14040	13036	11164	10164
9147	11157	12087	11161	9105	10147	14041	13037	11148	10148
9015	11232	12088	11220	9016	10149	14133	13038	11150	10150
9086	11209	12091	11207	9116	10151	14134	13039	11166	10152
9107	11149	12104	11151	9083	10153	14150	13040	11154	10154
9046	11189	12107	11167	9129	10155	14149	13041	11156	10156
9132	11217	12108	11219	9151	10157	14029	13042	11158	10158
9059	11205	12110	11159	9060	10159	14076	13043	11160	10160
9045	11086	12126	11229	9054	10161	14138	13044	11162	10162
9146	11233	12128	11234	9130	10145	14084	13045	11146	10146
10051	11052	13011	14018	10052	10168	11168	13046	14141	10167
10053	14033	13012	11054	10083	'10166	11147	13047	11152	10166
10087	14019	13013	11081	10088	10056	14123	13048	11170	10055
10070	14024	13014	11058	10064	10171	14027	13049	11172	10172
10067	11060	13015	14022	10068	10173	14095	13050	11197	10174
10061	14094	13016	11062	10062	10175	14130	13051	11190	10202
10063	14124	13017	11155	10058	10177	14077	13052	11178	10178
10065	14025	13018	11066	10066	10179	14122	13053	11180	10180
10059	11068	13019	14137	10060	10075	14121	13054	11084	10057
10069	11070	13020	14056	10072	10183	14085	13055	11184	10199
10071	14067	13021	11072	10054	10185	14055	13056	11186	10186
10073	14066	13022	11074	10074	10163	14052	13057	11188	10188
10191	11192	13023	14116	10192	10189	14065	13058	11176	10176
10077	14069	13024	11078	10078	10084	14053	13059	11076	10076
10079	14073	13025	11080	10080	10197	14028	13062	11198	10198
10081	11051	13026	14072	10082	10184	14064	13063	11200	10200
10085	14068	13027	11221	10086	10201	14080	13064	11202	10190
10181	11182	13028	14119	10182	10224	14081	13065	11204	10204
10169	14057	13029	11056	10170	10205	14090	13066	11206	10206

Spare Cars:
10203, 11064, 13070, 14153 (MF67D trailer with interior fans).
Line total: 354 cars

LINE 10 — 20 x MA52 (2-unit Articulated trains)
15 x 5-car trains type MF67A-D

‡E001:	†D01	C01	D02		E021:	†D41	C21	D42	
E002:	D03	C02	D04		E022:	D43	C22	D44	
E003:	†D05	C03	D06		E023:	†D45	C23	D46	
E004:	D07	C04	D08		E024:	D47	C24	D48	
E005:	†D09	C05	D10		E025:	†D49	C25	D50	
E006:	D11	C06	D12		E026:	D51	C26	D52	
E007:	†D13	C07	D14		E027:	†D53	C27	D54	
E008:	D15	C08	D16		E028:	D55	C28	D56	
E009:	†D17	C09	D18		E029:	†D57	C29	D58	
E010:	D19	C10	D20		E030:	D59	C30	D60	
E011:	†D21	C11	D22		E031:	†D61	C31	D62	
E012:	D23	C12	D24		E032:	D63	C32	D64	
E013:	†D25	C13	D26		E033:	†D65	C33	D66	
E014:	D27	C14	D28		E034:	D67	C34	D68	
‡E015:	†D29	C15	D30		E035:	†D69	C35	D70	
‡E016:	D31	C16	D32		E036:	D71	C36	D72	
E017:	†D33	C17	D34		‡E037:	†D73	C37	D74	
E018:	D35	C18	D36		E038:	D75	C38	D76	
‡E019:	†D37	C19	D38		E039:	†D77	C39	D78	
‡E020:	D39	C20	D40		E040:	D79	C40	D80	

†First class car.
‡Withdrawn from service.

MF67 Formations:

9029	11183	12039	11089	9053	9166	11211	12096	11139	9087
9092	11141	12046	11137	9148	9090	11193	12109	11087	9089
9063	11075	12047	11069	9152	9075	11191	12112	11185	9165
9091	11224	12050	11222	9070	9024	11215	12113	11135	9058
9030	11201	12077	11195	9156	9018	11231	12114	11065	9019
9074	11213	12080	11228	9041	9078	11061	12115	11073	9071
9110	11227	12082	11199	9131	9088	11083	12124	11085	9072
9017	11187	12092	11175	9158					

MA52 Service Train Formations:

E003 + E004	E009 + E010	E017 + E018	E025 + E026	E031 + E032	E035 + E036
E005 + E006	E011 + E012	E021 + E022	E027 + E028	E033 + E034	E039 + E040
E007 + E002	E013 + E014	E023 + E024	E029 + E030		

Spare Units:
E008, E038
Line total: 40 units (32 for service)
           75 cars

LINE 11 — 16 x 4-car trains type MP55
5 x 4-car trains type MP73

3002	5501	4001	3009	3018	5509	4009	3005
3015	5502	4002	3014	3030	5510	4005	3007
3008	5503	4011	3033	3031	5511	4008	3022
3035	5504	4012	3011	3010	5512	4010	3001
3003	5505	4017	3013	3027	5513	4016	3025
3021	5506	4018	3026	3029	5515	4006	3034
3032	5507	4004	3017	3023	5516	4007	3036
3012	5508	4015	3024	3006	5517	4003	3004
3503	6502	4502	3504	3509	6549	4505	3510
3511	6506	4506	3512	3507	7049	4504	3508
3513	6548	4507	3514				

Spare Cars:
3016, 3020, 4013, 5514
Line total: 88 cars

LINE 12 — 42 x 5-car trains type MF67A-D

9080	11109	12031	11012	9032	9162	11099	12097	11049	9021
9040	11015	12032	11027	9051	9020	11030	12098	11045	9027
9126	11114	12034	11216	9118	9077	11110	12099	11047	9028
9025	11025	12035	11026	9026	9115	11044	12100	11091	9100
9160	11117	12036	11104	9159	9112	11108	12101	11107	9035
9048	11120	12038	11102	9047	9145	11101	12103	11043	9082
9036	11092	12042	11024	9014	9163	11116	12105	11115	9138
9094	11046	12044	11125	9044	9037	11059	12106	11038	9065
9097	11017	12049	11103	9031	9052	11118	12116	11011	9013
9125	11112	12073	11002	9011	9134	11040	12117	11039	9135
9049	11100	12075	11018	9022	9067	11119	12118	11031	9106
9099	11029	12076	11032	9108	9064	11095	12120	11096	9137
9039	11093	12078	11111	9109	9055	11126	12121	11208	9153
9144	11105	12081	11033	9143	9081	11053	12122	11077	9069
9121	11042	12083	11021	9093	9066	11041	12123	11097	9139
9142	11014	12085	11023	9098	9034	11071	12125	11223	9033
9122	11016	12089	11128	9104	9062	11001	12127	11048	9084
9127	11022	12090	11037	9128	9111	11034	12129	11013	9133
9079	11036	12093	11113	9140	9061	11130	12130	11123	9095
9119	11020	12094	11122	9038	9050	11106	12131	11050	9120
9023	11028	12095	11035	9057	9096	11124	12132	11129	9161

Spare Cars:
9012, 9117, 11019, 11094, 11098, 11212, 12102
Line total: 217 cars

LINE 13 — 62 x 5-car trains type MF77

30001	32001	31001	32002	30002	30141	32141	31071	32142	30142
30010	32006	31003	32005	30006	30143	32143	31072	32144	30144
30007	32007	31004	32008	30008	30145	32145	31073	32146	30146
30009	32009	31005	32010	30005	30147	32147	31074	32148	30148
30011	32011	31006	32012	30012	30149	32149	31075	32150	30150
30013	32014	31007	32013	30014	30151	32151	31076	32152	30152
30015	32016	31008	32015	30016	‡30137	‡32137	31077	‡32138	‡30138
30017	32017	31009	32018	30018	30155	32155	31078	32156	30156
30019	32020	31010	32019	30020	†30157	32157	31079	32158	30158
30021	32021	31011	32022	30022	30221	32221	31111	32222	30222
30023	32024	31012	32023	30024	30295	32295	31148	32296	30296
30037	32037	31019	32038	30038	30297	32297	31149	32298	30298
30041	32041	31021	32042	30042	30299	32299	31150	32300	30300
30043	32043	31022	32044	30044	30301	32301	31151	32302	30302
30055	32056	31028	32055	30056	30303	32303	31152	32304	30304
30089	32089	31045	32090	30090	30305	32305	31153	32306	30306
30091	32091	31046	32092	30092	30307	32307	31154	32308	30308
30093	32093	31047	32094	30094	30309	32309	31155	32310	30310
30095	32095	31048	32096	30096	30311	32311	31156	32312	30312
30097	32097	31049	32098	30098	30313	32313	31157	32314	30314
30099	32099	31050	32100	30100	30315	32315	31158	32316	30316
30107	32107	31054	32108	30108	30375	32375	31188	32376	30376
30109	32109	31055	32110	30110	30377	32377	31189	32378	30378
30117	32117	31059	32118	30118	30379	32379	31190	32380	30380
†30153	32125	31063	32126	30126	30381	32381	31191	32382	30382
30127	32127	31064	32128	30128	30383	32383	31192	32384	30384
30129	32129	31065	32130	30130	30385	32385	31193	32386	30386
30131	32131	31066	32132	30132	30387	32387	31194	32388	30388
30133	32133	31067	32134	30134	30389	32389	31195	32390	30390
30135	32135	31068	32136	30136	30391	32391	31196	32392	30392
30139	32139	31070	32140	30140	30393	32393	31197	32394	30394

Spare Cars;
30125 (Asynchronous motors experiment), ‡31069
†Fitted with magnetic track brakes.
‡Fitted with white door push buttons.
Line total: 312 cars

Miscellaneous Stock

Eight five-car trains are kept for instructional purposes; three MF67A-D at Gare du Nord disused station on line 5 (9043-11165-12045-11063-9085, 10193-14148-13060-11194-10194 and 10195-14001-13061-11196-10196); one MF67CX at Porte de Charenton on line 8 (10225-11225-12119-11226-10226); one MF67A-E (10222-14307-13068-11121-10223) and one MF77 (30003-32003-31002-32004-30004) at the Gare de Lyon to Quai de la Rapée connection between lines 1 and 5; two MF67A-E at Villiers on line 3 (10221-14325-13072-11218-10227 and 10361-14331-13331-11331-10362); and one MP59/73 at Porte des Lilas disused station on the former shuttle line (3041-4034-7002-7047-3096).

Stock stored or out of service includes: 14352, 14353, 14356 (MF67E) at Auteuil depot on line 10; 13067, 13069, 13071 (MF67D) at Boulogne depot on line 9; 10003 (MF67W2) at Choisy depot on line 7; 11003-12002-11004-10004 (MF67W2) and 10338, 14314, 14326, 14328 (MF67E) at the line 6-8 connection at Daumesnil; 3019, 4014 (MP55) at Place d'Italie (line 6); 3028 (MP55) at the Sucy Experimental Centre; 7006, 7046 (MP73) at Château de Vincennes; 3599-6550-4550-3600, 3591-4546-6546-7046-3592 and 7050 (MP73) at Fontenay depot on line 1 (3599 and 3600 have prototype bogies of the type used on the Marseille Metro and for future RATP 'pneu' stock); 30411-11552-11553-30412 ('BOA' Prototype) on line 7bis under test.

In addition to the many vehicles of converted Sprague stock (motors and trailers) already mentioned, the RATP has other miscellaneous vehicles in its service stock fleet. These include diesel locomotives, a Plasser Track Maintenance machine, a 'Speno' Rail Grinding Train and various wagons for specialised work. In 1985-86, the RATP took delivery of 14 new Battery Locomotives ('TMA' - Tracteur à Marche Autonome - built by Alsthom). They have two cabs, one for normal driving, the other for shunting at low speeds, the batteries being located in the centre section of the locomotive, with an open-air gangway down the centre. It is likely that further 'TMA' locomotives will be built in the future, replacing the Sprague 'Tracteurs'.

Two battery/motor cars for engineers' trains (K01/02) were converted and rebuilt with KESAR equipment in 1973 using the chassis of Nord-Sud cars M2106 and M2108 and Jeumont equipment from motor cars M1149 and M1153.
Brian Hardy

Fourteen new battery locomotives were built by Alsthom in 1985–86 for works train duties – TMA02 is at Villette.
Brian Hardy

V290 built in 1970 by Etablissements Cadoux comprises a driving cab and is able to act as a driving trailer when formed in an engineers' train.
Brian Hardy

CHAPTER 6
FARES AND TICKETING

In times past, fare collection on the Métro was a labour-intensive operation. Due to the multiplicity of fares (1st and 2nd class tickets, return tickets, tickets extracted from booklets, weekly tickets, reduced fares, etc.), no automatic vending system could be contemplated until recent times. It was necessary to await the progress in electronics to solve the problem posed by such a complex fare structure at reasonable cost.

On the Métro, ticket checking has always been carried out at the start of a journey, supplemented by random checks on trains and in interchange corridors. Until 1973, control was by ticket examiners. Generally female, they were often referred to by Parisians as 'tricoteuses' (knitters) and they were reputed to be able to examine and punch 30 tickets a minute without dropping a stitch. Fare evasion, therefore, was virtually non-existent under their scrutiny!

The first automatic ticket checking system was installed at the time the first stage of the RER line A was opened to the public in 1969 and the RATP subsequently decided to equip the entire Métro system. However, the fact of the urban network being already in operation made it difficult to suddenly install definitive ticket checking machines. Moreover, it was necessary to gradually absorb the excess staff generated by automation. A transition period, therefore, saw the turnstiles unlocked by passengers themselves, by inserting an ordinary ticket in a type of machine that was already in use on the buses. By this means, an entire station could be fitted out without waiting for the design of computerised systems for processing magnetic tickets. Then, first in a few stations commencing on 8 October 1973, these ticket cancelling machines were replaced by magnetic ticket readers linked to a single data processing system, encompassing the entire urban Métro. By October the following year, the urban system had been completely re-equipped with magnetic ticket gates. Ticket offices not only print and issue tickets, but code them as well.

Insofar as fares on the Métro and RER are concerned, a unified system has been introduced encompassing all-in fares on all of the transit systems. Thus, the 'Carte Orange' (Orange Card), which is obtainable for varying periods, was devised jointly by the RATP and SNCF and was introduced from 1 July 1975. Not even the most enthusiastic advocates of the Carte Orange could have foreseen its success, it being held by about 1.8-million passengers, and accounting for some 49% of all trips made on the Métro. There are five Carte Orange ticketing zones around Paris, zone 1 being the area within the City boundary, and so on, working outwards. For the Métro, zone 2 covers the sections beyond the boundary, except for five extreme ends of lines, which go into zone 3. These are: Carrefour Pleyel to Saint-Denis-Basilique (line 13), La Courneuve and the three Villejuif stations (line 7), both Bobigny stations (line 5) and Alfort-Ecole Vétérinaire to Créteil-Préfecture (line 8).

Publicity: The Success of 'Le Ticket'
Neither the CMP nor the RATP made many efforts to develop a house style for use on posters or in publicity material. The result of this was shown by a survey made in 1973 which revealed that, while most Parisians held a personal view of the buses and the Métro, they were totally vague about the RATP itself. It was decided to remedy this situation, in parallel with the improvements to the Métro system generally, and with the alterations then being made to ticketing.

The first publicity campaigns were purely informative and were linked to developments such as automatic ticketing or the modernisation of stations, and though successful enough, did not raise public awareness of the system as a whole, nor did they reach those who were not using public transport. The launch of the 'Carte Orange' was seized upon as an opportunity to promote the use of RATP services as an alternative to the car and in 1978 this campaign concentrated on the theme of the 'second car'. It depended on rational arguments and eschewed the fantasy of London Transport, which put a tube train into a suburban garage – perhaps for that reason it was unsuccessful. A second campaign associated the users of public transport with trendy activities such as jogging, and was rather better received, but the motorists in general still stayed in their cars.

What was in fact still lacking was a brand image for the RATP and its services, and in 1981 a solution, brilliant in its simplicity, was conceived. The brand image would be the ticket, the ordinary yellow and brown Métro ticket. A pre-test showed that this could go down very well with the public. Starting with the 'second car' campaign, the ticket featured in successive campaigns where it was associated with articles such as Levi jeans and Lacoste shirts, the idea being to convey an image of taste and comfort, laced with a dash of snob-appeal. The campaign was backed by a short film 'Ticket Chic, Ticket Choc', which won considerable acclaim in the media, and the music from which became a hit single. Since then the ticket has been the star of many publicity campaigns and has assumed many forms – a violin, a tennis racquet, ballet shoes and other fantasies. Occasionally, the images verged on the surreal, as when the ticket became a Star of Bethlehem at Christmas 1982 (presumably wise men travel by the RATP), but there is no doubt that the ticket has imprinted the RATP and its facilities firmly on the commercial life of the capital. In 1983 the Poster Museum ran a special exhibition in honour of the campaign, the publicity for which 'Le Musée à la ticket' won the annual prize for the best French poster.

Building on this success, the RATP has opened, at Châtelet-les-Halles RER station, a boutique selling a wide variety of souvenirs featuring the ticket in some form or another, and the visitor who would like to take home with him a reminder of a trip to Paris can choose anything between an umbrella and a pen, a towel and a mug – or he can simply keep a ticket!

To reduce the amount of fraudulent travel on the Métro, new and replacement AFC installations include gates that cannot be jumped over. This view was taken in 1981 at La Chapelle station on line 2.

R.J. Greenaway

ABBREVIATIONS USED:

Companies/Organisations

AMTUIR	Association pour le Musée des Transports Urbains, Interurbains et Rureaux
CMP	Compagnie de Chemin de Fer Métropolitain de Paris
EDF	Electricité de France
NS (or Nord-Sud)	Société de Chemin de Fer Électrique Souterrain Nord-Sud de Paris
ORTP	Office Régional des Transports Parisiens
RATP	Régie Autonome des Transports Parisiens
RER	Réseau Express Régional
SNCF	Société National de Chemin de Fer
STCRP	Société des Transports en Commun de la Région Parisienne
STP	Syndicat des Transports Parisiens

Rolling Stock/Equipment Manufacturers

Alsthom	Société Alsthom-Atlantique
ANF	Ateliers du Nord de la France à Blanc Misseron
BL	Brissonneau et Lotz
CAFL	Compagnie des Acieries et Forges de la Loire
CEM	Compagnie Electro-Méchanique
CGT	Compagnie Générale de Traction
CIMT	Compagnie Industrielle de Matériel de Transport
Creusot Loire	Société Creusot Loire
Düwag	Düsseldorfer Waggonfabrik
JH	Jeumont-Heidmann
Jeumont	Société Jeumont-Schneider
MTE	Société Matériel Traction Électrique
RNUR	Régie Nationale des Usines Renault
SFB	Société Franco Belge, subsequently Société Ferroviaire du Valenciennes (SOFERVAL)
TCO	Société de Traction CEM Oerlikon

Equipment/Systems

AIMT	Automobilisation Integrale du Movement des Trains
ATO	Automatic Train Operation (English version). French equivalent – Pilotage Automatique
CMC	Conduite Manuelle Contrôlée
PCC	Poste de Commande Centralisée
PCE	Poste de Commande d'Energie

Rolling Stock Types

MA	Matériel Articulé
MF	Matériel Fer
MP	Matériel Pneu

Rolling Stock Vehicle Types

M	Driving Motor car 2nd class (Motrice avec loge, deuxieme classe)
Bb	Second class trailer (Remorque deuxieme classe) – Sprague & Nord-Sud stock only
Ab	First class trailer (Remorque premiere classe) – Sprague & Nord-Sud stock only
B	Second class trailer (Remorque deuxieme classe)
A	First class trailer (Remorque premiere classe)
AB	Composite trailer (Remorque mixte)
N	Non-driving motor car, 2nd class (Motrice sans loge, deuxieme classe)
NA	Non-Driving motor car, 1st class (Motrice sans loge, premiere classe)
S	Driving trailer, 2nd class (Remorque avec loge conduite, deuxieme classe)
T	Works train driving motor car (Tracteurs)
TA	Depot shunting driving motor Car (Tracteurs Ateliers)
V	Miscellaneous vehicles (Véhicles auxiliare)
VX	Special miscellaneous vehicles (Véhicles Spéciaux)
TMA	Battery Locomotive (Tracteur à Marche Autonome)
E	Unit (Element)

THE FOLLOWING PUBLICATIONS WERE USEFUL IN THE COMPILATION OF THIS HANDBOOK:
ON RAILS UNDER PARIS (B. J. Prigmore, LRTL 1974). ENTRE LES LIGNES
NOTRE METRO (J. Robert, 1983). RAILWAY GAZETTE INTERNATIONAL
LA VIE DU RAIL Numerous RATP documents.